Beyond Me

Practices for
Expanding Compassion

by

David T. Weibel, Ph.D.

Compassion Publishing
2546 Hundred Oaks Avenue
Baton Rouge, LA 70808

Cover design and graphics and fish drawings by Marissa Padilla

Library of Congress Control Number: 2015913565

Weibel, David

Beyond Me: Practices for Expanding Compassion
David T. Weibel, – 1st Compassion Publishing hardcover ed.
includes bibliographical references.

ISBN
978-0-9897904-2-0
978-0-9897904-4-4 (ebook)

Pages 198, cm 15 x 23

Printed and bound in the United States of America

1   2   3   4   5   6   7   8   9   10

Acknowledgements

I would like to offer deepest gratitude to the following: The teachers, the ones who taught me directly, the ones who taught my teachers, and the original teachers, including Buddha, Lao Tzu, and Jesus, and all their followers including Alan Watts, Lama Surya Das, Thomas Merton, Pema Chödrön, Jack Kornfield, D. T. Suzuki, Thich Nhat Hanh, and Tenzin Gyatso.

My graduate school advisor Timothy Anderson, therapy mentors John Garske and Paula Andrassi, and those I know best from books, such as Yalom, Rogers, Maslow, and Kabat-Zinn. Scholarship guides such as Sam Harris, Jean Twenge, Stephen Pinker, Ken Wilber, Kristin Neff, and Robert Wright.

Compassion Publishing, especially Spencer Ware.

My psychotherapy clients - I cherish the privilege of hearing your stories.

Stan Drake, Physical Education master, who taught the joy of no-look passes. Gary Riekes, master of human development, who is a beloved mentor to thousands of young people.

Friends who have shared the compassion path including John Pickering, Patrick Hanlin, Francisco Lopez, Ian McCarthy, Joseph Austin, Thomas Gotsch, Brian Uhlin, Edgar Wing, Christine Catura, Brian Kinnaird, Tom Knoblauch, Michael Bek, Kimberly Stanard, Gene Hwang, Stan Otani, Simone Kytle, Eric Doyle, Vann Miller, Laurie Fox, Janet Roberts, and Andrew Sammons.

"The Boys" of younger days, and their associates.

Linda Weibel, Harry Stevens, Dale Weibel, Patricia Goss, Stephen Weibel, Erin Hayes, Max Mayer, Jena Mayer, Geoff Goss, Jennifer Goss, Dalmen Mayer, Carol Weibel, Mike, Mark, Kim, Paul, Dean & Donna Weibel, and the Coyles.

To the better half, Erin Coyle, an incredibly wise and supportive person. And Caelen, who helps me to expand beyond me in a classic way, by loving him more than my self.

*To the helpers, coyotes,
and mystics in training
who lighten the mood and the self.*

I

The Dissatisfied Self

II

Compassion Practices

Expanding Me

Preface

Hi, Monkey. Yes, you. You act like a monkey. At least your mind does. Jumping to and fro, grasping, and rarely sitting still. Your monkey mind's favorite topic is itself, and the vast majority of your suffering occurs because you generate endless thoughts about your self. You worry about what will happen to you and then become frustrated when the world does not comply with what your ego had in mind. To escape the self's constant evaluation and criticism, you self-medicate, or medicate the self, numbing or distracting the mind by engaging in the overs: over-eating, drinking, sexing, drugging, controlling, gambling, shopping, or exercising. The component of mind we all try to escape is me, my ego, the self. The self needs to chill.

This book is a playful journey toward taking a break from your troubles, or the troubles that you imagine to be an essential part of you. What exactly is the self we are going to expand or get beyond? Well, your body will still be here. It is far too useful for dancing. The part or the process of the self that we want to expand, transcend, or simply quiet, is the craving, striving, clinging, judging, self-focused, self-absorbed, dis-satisfied, discontented, hyperactive ego within us all. If you have already noticed this ego creature, then you have begun the journey.

How can you move beyond me, quieting the self? Begin by noticing. Just as a fish does not notice the water in which it swims, we often do not notice our mind's perpetual background noise. Pay attention to your everyday mind. Realize how often you are in the self-conscious and self-focused mode, as opposed to being mode, in which you are fully immersed in your experience.

Also notice the best moments of your life and have more of them. What you will likely notice is that there is no you in your best moments. Specifically, there is no awareness of self or self-consciousness in those moments. Your body is there. Your senses and your being are there. Yet, self-consciousness, the self as the focus of awareness, is absent. While you were enjoying a beautiful sunset, your mind probably was not thinking, "How am I performing?" Instead, your being was fully immersed in the sunset, experiencing it. You were not identified with your ego or any thing. There was no self, or self-consciousness, and no need for self-focused chatter. This book is about expanding our selves to get beyond our little ego stories, and getting into our lives, the experience of life. A major tool to help us get beyond our selves is to take them less seriously. Another vehicle is to practice compassion.

The Oxford dictionary defines compassion as sympathetic pity and concern for the sufferings or misfortunes of others. This definition is helpful but not wide enough for our purposes, as it focuses only on suffering and mainly on feelings. The form of compassion we recommend is wider. For our purposes, compassion involves a set of attitudes, thoughts, and feelings that are fostered by cultural evolution, empathy, and reasoning and allow us to act in ways that minimize others' suffering and maximize their thriving and joy. The modern capacity for compassion has been influenced by the evolution of the species, such as the human frontal lobes that allow behavioral inhibition and reasoning, as well as cultural evolution, such as the rights revolutions which now make it increasingly obvious to a growing number of people that all races, genders, ages, sexual orientations, and sometimes even all species have rights and deserve equal or at least fair treatment. When a culture becomes more compassionate, it does raise all or at least most boats. An individual's compassion also depends on their genetics and their ability to practice and develop skills in perspective taking, reasoning, empathy, and altruism.

The compassion practices in this book, which are time tested via ancient wisdom and modern science, will help us realize higher consciousness and wider empathy. We are going to dance and play our way through compassion practices, expanding our hearts, opening our minds, and moving beyond me.

How to read the book

However you want. Except, please do Exercise #1 two pages from here first, and then let loose. A major objective of this book is to develop a flexible self, so you can move where you feel drawn or choose a chapter at random. Part I describes problems with the self and Part II explains how to transcend these.

Warning: Part I might be a bit of a downer. It is a realistic exploration of how the self contributes to suffering. Part II is far happier. If you already know that ego is an obstacle and want optimistic tools for self-liberation, jump to Part II. You may still want to revisit Part I at some point, because a fuller understanding of how the self evolved and how it operates will help you understand others and transcend the self. To maximize flow and readability, references and notes are at the end of the book rather than listed throughout the text.

Because the book is about moving beyond me, the author will remain mostly behind the scenes, using the first person infrequently and telling few personal anecdotes. This book will occasionally bend spelling and grammar rules, just as it aims to loosen beliefs that have limited your self. He or she constructions will not be used. To point out the self's thinginess, we will sometimes split words such as ourselves. Sometimes we will use we when we could use I, the author. There is only one writer; the we means all his many selves as well as all his influences.

This book is intended to be both humorous and challenging. The humor is designed to help you take your self less seriously; the challenges are designed to snap you out of self-obsession. Please enjoy both and do not take the author, nor your self, too seriously.

Please do the following exercise before moving on to any other part of the book. Like virginity, you will never get a second chance.

Exercise # 1

Use your computer to write a story about what happened in the previous two weeks, writing at least 250 words. Then, use the word count feature to delete words until you have exactly 250.

If you skipped it, please go back and do the exercise on the previous page.

Please go back to your story and count the number of personal pronouns ("I, me, my, mine"). How many did you have? Dr. Larry Scherwitz, examining the risk factors for coronary heart disease, found that people who were the most self-focused (those who referred to themselves using the pronouns "I", "me" and "my" most often in an interview) were more likely to develop coronary heart disease, even when other health-threatening behaviors were controlled for (Scherwitz & Ornish, 1994)[1]. One interpretation for this study is that self-focused people are less healthy, and are more likely to develop heart disease.

The instructions to Exercise 1 were to write about what happened in the previous two weeks. The instructions did not say to write about you. People can write about anything: their day, their friends, or local or global news. Most people choose to write from first person (I, me). It is ok. There is nothing wrong with you if you had "I's", "me's", or "my's." After all, you are both the main character and the writer of your life.

However, you might ask whether it might be more relaxing to be more other-focused and less me-focused.

---

[1]Please do not feel bad if you had many *me's*. You could have been in a *me* mood. Also, realize that the counting *me's* exercise was not a pure experiment. You may have guessed where the experiment was going, and thus used few *me's*. The study was correlational, so it is not easy to tease apart causality. It could be that people who are ill focus more on their selves, not that self-focus causes illness. However, both possibilities can be entertained. This study was mainly offered as a modern research example of what the wisdom traditions already know. The best of the ancient wisdom agrees that ego is the obstacle to spiritual growth, peace, and health and that transcending ego is the road to contentment.

We can ask how much of our mental activity is self-absorbed or self-focused and whether we always talk about our self if someone asks what is happening. If you usually respond in a self-focused manner, notice if constant self-concern raises your stress. Notice if you get a little break from your self when you think about your dog, watch a sunset, or dance.

Western research has begun to consider the idea that self-focus and self-absorption could be the cause of psychological problems, disorders and illness, rather than simply being a personality variable or a symptom. The wisdom and spiritual traditions have large bodies of first-person evidence from contemplative scientists[2] and a large degree of agreement among the traditions that too much ego or self-absorption is the main struggle that humans must overcome in their journey to realize higher consciousness and lasting happiness.

The premise of this book is that constantly thinking in me-mode is quite stressful and boring, and that this mode of thinking has never been more prominent in the history of the planet, or causing more damage.

---

[2] The term contemplative scientist refers to monks and other dedicated meditators who have practiced for decades to develop their consciousness and refine their tools of introspection. They collect data via their experience in a systematic manner and then present this data to a community of the qualified, the other monks, and help refine the body of knowledge.

I

The Dissatisfied Self

1

Why Me?

The Oxford Dictionary defines self as "a person's essential being that distinguishes them from others, especially when considered as the object of introspection or reflexive action." This self sounds fairly harmless, and this book does not aim to obliterate all aspects of self. When we say *transcend the self*, we mean to move beyond certain thoughts, beliefs, attitudes, ways of perceiving, and properties of mind. The phrase *transcend the self* does not mean to upload your brain into a computer and leave your body behind. We are not trying to get rid of our bodies; they are too useful for playing drums.

To transcend the self does not mean to obliterate it. Ken Wilber coined the phrase "transcend and include." A higher level of consciousness includes any lower levels and does not destroy them. The most enlightened and peaceful person could still call upon reptilian violent instincts if a criminal was attacking her family. Whatever we transcend, we can still access if the need arises.

Whenever we say transcend the self, shrink the self, move beyond me, quiet ego, transcend ego, expand consciousness, expand compassion, or reach higher consciousness, we are talking about the same process. Use whichever terms suit your fancy. We are going to name the part of the self that we want to transcend or move beyond, the Dissatisfied Self. The Dissatisfied Self refers to the entrenched habits of the mind to believe that it is the permanent owner and driver of one's life, and to engage in constant self-referential thinking in which it reviews and judges its performance and image in the past and worries about its performance and image in the future, thus prohibiting the experience of being fully aware in the present moment.

The Dissatisfied Self refers to the habits of the mind to believe:

1. My self is permanent.

2. My self is the owner, driver, and boss of this life.

3. My self needs to constantly review and judge its performance and image in the past and worry about its performance and image in the future.

4. My self has no time for the present; it needs to
review and prepare.

The Dissatisfied Self believes I am a permanent, rigid
identity that remains the same across all situations, and
that I also need to protect my self against all possible
dangers, both real and imagined. The Dissatisfied Self is
constantly evaluating the object of me against a set of
expectations, and taking on self-improvement projects to
ward off any and all possible future threats and to satisfy
a bottomless pit of cravings. Via self-conscious thinking,
the Dissatisfied Self is frequently monitoring, checking,
judging, and criticizing, because it thinks these thinking
habits improve its chance of survival. The Dissatisfied
Self is a thought addict, and it is annoying. It needs a
vacation. First a hug, because it is weak and afraid, and
then a vacation.

To understand the Dissatisfied Self, we need to
understand an opposite style of existing. Terms to
describe the opposite of the Dissatisfied Self include
mindfulness, experiencing, and being. These terms are
near enough to each other to be used as synonyms.
Mindfulness is paying attention the present moment in an
accepting manner. This simple definition implies a great
deal. If we are accepting the moment, we are not judging
it, nor trying to change it. If we are fully present and
accepting, we are free of self-focused thought and all
unnecessary mental chatter. Recall the best sunset you
ever saw. Your mind did not need to chatter about it.
Eyes receive visual stimuli. The mind experiences. No
thoughts needed. Any thought might have been minimal,
such as "Beautiful" or "Ahh." The Dissatisfied Self can
ruin potential mindful moments, even when we are totally

safe and on vacation. Self-conscious chatter during the sunset would be, "I love this. This ranks among my best sunsets." As soon as evaluations emerge, grasping and clinging will follow. As soon as you rank it highly, you will want to hold it and duplicate it tomorrow, creating expectations and striving.

The mindful, non ego-focused mind state has also been called experiencing, meaning that we are fully present in our bodies, feeling whatever is occurring in the moment without self-focused mental commentary, and really without any commentary. Think about the best dancing you have ever done or ever will do. You are totally in the flow of the music, connecting with your partner, and merging with the vibe of the room. You do not need to think "This is the best dancing I've done!" in your partner's ear or even in your own head. The thought track is not even "I'm having an experience." It's just experiencing. An experience. Your thoughts and commentary are not needed. Stop the word spew and dance.

Another word that has been used to describe the mindful or experiencing state is being. Being is sometimes contrasted with doing or forcing. In being mode there is no resistance, forcing, or even trying. While being, there is plenty of letting go and allowing to be. Being frees us from forcing or trying too hard, letting us practice effortless effort as the Taoists would say. While being, we are in the moment, not labeling it, resisting it, or trying to improve it. We are not trying to get to some other place or moment. Just be.

The hallmarks of mindfulness, experiencing, or being are full presence in this moment with openness and acceptance. As soon as you are not accepting, you are not fully experiencing the moment. Judging or even commenting on the moment will take you out of the moment. Mindfulness is receiving, not judging. In contemplative traditions overreliance on definitions, categories, and the literal mind, the word machine, can be an obstacle. The terms mindful, being, or experiencing can be treated as interchangeable. Use whichever word resonates. The words are not the thing. Words will never capture the experience. They are merely pointers.[3] Buddhist teachers have long told students that a finger pointing at the moon is not the moon. The map is not the territory. Pixels in a later part of this book will encourage the collection of processes that goes by the name your parents gave it, to drop the book and experience.

---

[3] Print or Pixels- symbols decoded by your eyes. Reading is certainly helpful, but no one learns to dance via reading.

	Dissatisfied Self	Being Mode
	Self-conscious Self-focused Self-absorbed	Mindful Aware Experiencing
<u>Situation</u> Viewing a sunset	"This is the best sunset." "This would be better if I was with _____." "I better enjoy this; it might get cold soon."	Experienced, not described. "Beautiful"
At a party	"Do I look good?" "They are cooler/ less cool than me." "I'm missing a better party."	Immersed
During the game	"How am I playing?" "I must play better."	Letting the body take over = *Flow* "Ball."
Making love	"How does my _____ look?" "Am I doing this well?"	Pleasure "Yes!"

The mindful side of the chart on the previous page could have had even fewer thoughts, but the chart called for a few examples to communicate to the reader. We have now established an overview of the difference between mindless and mindful living, between self-conscious and being modes. You may have noticed long ago that the best moments in your life are mindful moments. Part II of this book is dedicated to helping us move beyond me to experience our lives. The remainder of Part I will detail how the Dissatisfied Self forms and why it is an obstacle to our compassion and happiness.

2

Where Do I Come From?

You arrive from the perfect temperature hot tub to the shock of blinding light, cold, and noise. However, things are still pretty good. In your baby mind, the world serves you. In fact, it is you. You and the world are one. In your baby mind, Mom's breast is no different than your hand. You cry; she provides. The arrival of Mom's breast feels like scratching an itch feels now. You as a baby thought you owned and controlled Mom in a similar manner as the adult you controls your hand. And at first you are not that good at scratching or eating, so it is very helpful to have these self-extensions, parents, to do your bidding.

This state of oneness, oceanic bliss, or limitless connectedness is quite pleasurable. Some theorists say the entire spiritual journey is a lifelong quest to return to this state of oneness. So why not just stay there, in the state of oneness? Why do you have to come out of the bliss of limitless narcissism ("I am the world"), do all the work of growing up, to then pursue spiritual practice trying to get a glimpse of this apparently complete connectedness?

First, it is a developmental necessity to realize that you are separate. Second, the connectedness of a baby and a spiritually enlightened person are quite different. The connectedness of the baby involves believing or acting as if everything is an extension of you (limitless narcissism). The connectedness from a spiritual quest involves realizing one is part of an interconnected web, and not more or less important than other parts. The limitless narcissism of the baby is more narrow, primitive, and simple than spiritual enlightenment, though they share a feeling of connectedness, the absence of separateness.

Developmentally, we need to realize that Mom and others are separate beings, separate people. Imagine you have not yet separated and individuated, and still thought everything was a part of you. You are at daycare, feeling somewhat thirsty, and you see your voluptuous teacher walking by your desk. Thinking she is still an extension of you, you reach out for some nourishment. This would likely be problematic. It is useful to realize that others exist; they have degrees of separateness from one's self; and they likely do not want to be groped during story time.

So the development of a self is necessary to avoid groping the teacher. Later it helps with career planning. Having an understanding of who you are, what you like, and whom you want to date is tremendously helpful. The ability to see one's self in the future and to plan for this future is one of the main reasons we are the dominant species on the planet. The ability to use our own self as a reference point when considering other selves and empathizing with their perspectives is perhaps what makes us most human. So we do not want to stop or eliminate the process of identity-formation. We want to understand the self, keep the necessary and useful facets, and then transcend ego, moving toward wider consciousness.

3

How Does the Self Help Us?

Assume for a moment that you live in a society that has abolished personal identities. You are teaching third grade, and none of the twenty-three children in your class have a name, because the culture has decided that names are an elitist form of oppression. Grading might be a little tough, as would be getting the girl who would have been called Huxley to stop pulling the hair of the boy who would have been called Caelen. Names as well as identities help others find and know us, and are an organizing principle among social groups.

Deciding

Imagine walking down the cereal aisle if you had no preferences. When a child first visits the cereal aisle, their little arms reach, pointing at every sugary delight. The child is in heaven as long as you do not make them purchase something too healthy. But make them choose only one cereal and choose quickly, and they will sweat bullets.

Researchers studying the influence of options on choice went into grocery stores and offered one group of shoppers a coupon and free tastings of six jams and another group of shoppers a coupon and free tastings of twenty-four jams. The researchers had hypothesized that people would buy more jam with twenty-four choices than with six. Most people equate choice as a benefit, thinking that if they had more choices, they could find their ideal jam, matching their unique preferences, and then make a purchase. The same principle applies with cars or mates. We assume that if we have more options we would find the perfect mate.[4] However, the researchers found that people bought far more jam when offered six choices rather than twenty-four choices. Choice can overwhelm, or more precisely, too much choice overwhelms.

Because choice is everywhere and deciding is frequently difficult, it helps to have a self that has preferences, tendencies, and habits. The ego's rigidity can be an obstacle in spiritual practice, but an aide when deciding between sugary delights in the cereal aisle. Imagine if every time you walked in the grocery store, you not only had no list, you had no sense of self and no preferences to help you choose. You would not know where to start. Having a self with preferences will be even more important when deciding on friends, a career, or a mate.

Establishing a Role within the Community

Roles and identities help others help us. When you want to organize a soccer game, you invite your friends who enjoy the identity of fútbolista. When you are in first grade and want to play kickball at recess, you start your pitch with the most kickball-friendly people. Once your friends know that you live to play kickball, you will have more kickball related information and events directed toward you. Your own attention will also be directed toward your preferences, increasing the likelihood that

---

[4] A person could reason that if they had more lovers to choose from, eventually they would find true love. Yet, the strategy of 'I will date everyone until I meet the perfect other' seems a recipe for perpetual singlehood.

you see kickball related information. Later your identity
might even help with dating when people try to set you
up on dates. If your friends know you love Costa Rican
snowboarders, they will likely search through their mental
roster of Costa Ricans and/or snowboarders to try and
find a person who might meet your preferences.

Planning & Delay of Gratification

The self helps us imagine possible selves in the future
and envision the pros and cons of today's behavior on
our future. By projecting this thing called me into the
future, and envisioning possible future selves, your
current self is able to delay today's gratifications to work
toward future gratifications your future selves might
receive.

While planning, we also likely consider how the
results of our planning will impact others. If you lived
alone in woods, you would plan for firewood and cabin
maintenance. But the vast majority of us are social
animals, and the importance of planning increases once
we consider our community. So while planning, you likely
consider, "If I invest four, six, or ten years in college,
who will I be? What will I be able to do? And how will
others react to me?" We plan, not only to survive, but to
thrive as social animals.

Some selves choose a slow and steady approach, such
as pursuing education, promotions, or investments. Some
selves choose a high risk, potential high reward strategy,
such as becoming a drug kingpin or rock star. Many male
rock stars admit that they started their band from a love
of music and to lure ladies, along with acceptance,
admiration, and hopefully, money in the future. If the

aspiring drug kingpin could not envision their future self receiving the accoutrements of power, they would not have been willing to engage in the high risk and long struggles to climb the criminal pyramid. If you cannot envision your future self reaping the rewards of your efforts, you likely cannot delay gratification long enough to engage in long struggles. Consider chimps with whom we share much DNA. Without belittling their existing abilities, let us admit that chimps do not appear to think, "Wait. If I study hard, I will get into grad school, learn advanced fruit-discovery, become main chimp, and lure all the ladies."

Perspective Taking

The self helps us to take on others' perspectives, which is the key to empathy, compassion, and higher consciousness. Perspective taking is perhaps the most important function of the self, and the one we are going to expand to get beyond me. Empathy can emerge because we know how it feels to have a self that experiences a whole range of thoughts and emotions. We remember experiences, particularly those charged with emotion, that were important for our selves. The ability to read other people's thoughts and emotions depends on fully knowing and remembering how my self has thought and felt in situations, imagining how my self would think and feel in other situations, and then extrapolating to imagine how the other would think or feel in potential situations. The ability to consider how another feels allows us to understand and better meet the needs of friends we would like to have and spouses we would like to keep. It should help our leaders consider the feelings and perspectives of people in other countries that would make better allies than enemies.

A rapidly growing body of research is showing that we are hard-wired for empathy and that the beginnings of perspective taking and empathy occur early in life. Mirror neurons in the brain come on-line early and fire whenever we imitate people. Babies will cry when they hear other babies cry, and it does not appear to be because of the noise. Noise will not make a baby cry as often as crying by a real baby, nor fake-crying by a computer. Babies cry when they hear babies who are upset. When toddlers see a person in pain (or simulated pain), such as after banging a knee, they will soothe the injured person, often via touch.

If an adult drops a pen on purpose, the baby looks mildly puzzled but does not react. However, if the experimenter appears to accidentally drop the pen, and reaches for it, while adding a disappointed, "Oops," the baby immediately crawls for the pen, in an effort to help. To do this, the baby has to take the other's perspective and understand that it is annoying when you drop things, unintentionally that is.

In another study design, babies watch movies in which one shape (e.g., a circle) is climbing up a hill when another shape will push against the circle, hindering it, and then a third shape helps by pushing on the circle's back as it tries to make it up the slope. After witnessing the movie, six-month old infants reached for the helping shape over the hindering shape, demonstrating a preference. It appears young babies prefer helpful individuals. The babies must demonstrate perspective taking to place their mind in the 'mind' of the circle shape trying to get up the hill and appreciate the help of the helpful shape, while resenting the hindrance of the hindering shape. With a similar study design, children as young as three months old showed a preference for the helping shape by looking longer at the helping shape.

In another study design, a puppet struggles to lift the lid on a box. A helpful puppet assists with lifting the lid and opens it all the way, while an antisocial jerk puppet jumps on the box and slams it shut. In another version, the first puppet is playing with a ball when it rolls away. The helpful puppet rolls the ball back while the puppet with a death-wish grabs the ball and runs away.[5] In both situations five-month olds prefer the helper, the good guy.

In an extension of the lid-slamming and ball-stealing puppets, researchers asked 21-month olds to give a treat to one of the two puppets (helper, hinderer) and to take away a treat from one. The babies gave treats to the helpful puppet and took one away from the hindering puppet. This sheds some light on the development of punishment, but it also illuminates the origins of empathy. Before punishing, the baby has to take the perspective of the puppet that was trying to get the box lid open or play with the ball.

While we may have an innate potential for empathy, empathy takes time to fully develop, and people vary widely in their empathic capacities. A pre-requisite for empathy is theory of mind. Theory of mind is the ability to be aware of and interpret one's own mind as well as

---

[5] I'm being playful. If you steal any of my balls, I hope you can run fast. Taking a ball is a heinous offense. Lil' help (a little help) is a universal phrase for a ball that has rolled off the field toward a passersby. It is the passersby's duty to chase and return the ball, preferably with enough skill to show they could join the game.

other's thoughts, beliefs, emotions, and perspectives and to know that they are not necessarily the same.

Studies have shown that people vary on their levels of perspective taking and theory of mind based on age and development as well due to certain traits or conditions that have a genetic influence. A classic false belief experiment involves two research participants looking at and trying to locate an object such as keys under one of two boxes. Imagining yourself in the experiment, you and the other participant are looking at two open-bottomed boxes on a table. The experimenter places a set of keys under one box. The other participant is asked to leave the room. While she is gone, the experimenter moves the keys from under one box to the other. The experimenter then asks you, "Where do you think the other participant [the person who left the room] will look for the keys?" Here is the amazing finding. Children under four years of age, and people of all ages who fall in the autistic spectrum[6], more frequently answer that the other participant will look for the keys where the keys currently are, the 2nd box, the location to which you, but not the other participant, saw the experimenter move them. The setup is too innocent to suspect duplicity on the part of the researcher. The young person without a well-developed theory of mind thinks the other person,

---

[6] Autism is a serious condition that deserves far more research and treatment funding. The situation of people living with autism is not cleanly analogous to a non-autistic person with low empathy or to a narcissistic person. The experiments on theory of mind do provide an example of how people can vary widely in their ability to take other's perspectives based on their own genetics or their age and level of development. Exploring theory of mind and empathy across the autism spectrum as well as among the entire population is a rich research area.

and in fact the whole world, *sees what I see*, understands the world as I see it. Without a fully formulated or well-developed theory of other minds, the only mind, view, or perspective that I perceive well is mine. Within the experiment, a person lacking in theory of mind has trouble considering that the participant will most likely look for the keys were she last saw the keys, under the first box, where they were before they were covertly moved.

This simple experiment has profound implications if we use our powers of extrapolation and consider the experiment as an analogy or lens into how perspective taking and empathy can effect every human interaction. If I am in that experiment with limited perspective taking abilities, I believe the person who left the room will think the keys are where I saw them being moved, as the world knows everything I know, for it is the only truth I can conceptualize. I cannot imagine being behind their eyes. The keys experiment deals with basic facts, the location of keys. Think of how much more complexity is involved in trying to understand someone's perspective or emotions about a complex issue.

Regarding politics, we often think that if others have full access to the information and adequate deductive powers, they will likely reach the same conclusion as us. The complete disbelief we experience when others do not vote like us, is similar to the child in the experiment who does not understand why the other participant does not know where the keys are, in their new location. We are not able to understand how those others "did not see the keys being moved." They have a different view or angle than us. We are not in the same seat. This might help explain simple relationship failures in addition to problems we have considering the mindset of those who are different than us, whether men, women, old, young, parents, children, liberals, or conservatives. Seeing the angle or view of our opponents or enemies is even more difficult.

Luckily, having a self helps us to engage in hypotheticals, mental simulations, and pretend or make-believe scenarios. For example, having a self is foundational requirement to consider possibilities such as, "How would my friend feel if their child died?" or "How would my husband feel if I cheated?" Without a self, without a theory of mind, and the ability to take perspectives, we cannot imagine what another self might feel. This ability to engage in hypotheticals, which frequently use the conditional and subjunctive verb tenses, is an advanced thinking skill that some people never master.

Try learning another language. You will find the conditional and subjunctive tenses to be difficult. It is not only because of the newness or difficulty of the language. It is because of the complexity in mental operations implied by hypotheticals that use the subjunctive tense, 'What would have happened if you would have dared to kiss him rather than simply say goodnight?', 'If you were to tell her how you feel the next time you see her, what would happen?' This is both complex grammar and complex thinking involving time frames and perspective taking. The ability to consider our selves in 'what if' hypothetical scenarios also helps us to consider the other in the same scenarios. This perspective taking is the basis for empathy, emotional intelligence, and compassion.

Summary

We have reviewed how the self is necessary to help us decide, plan, delay gratification, and take on the perspectives of others, so that we can thrive as social creatures. Early in childhood we certainly need to form some concept of self-awareness. A self is helpful when choosing between chocolate or vanilla, guitar or drums, or a hike or a swim. A self is helpful when planning what career you want to pursue or who you want to marry. Despite its usefulness, the self is not content to merely serve its useful functions; it grows and becomes increasingly active until it dominates our waking moments. Now we will explore how the potentially useful self, once entrenched and solidified, launches a hostile takeover of our awareness, and mutates into the Dissatisfied Self, causing us pain.

4

Watching My Back

I am always vigilant, even when there is nothing there.

Close your eyes and try to focus on your breathing for five minutes. You will notice your mind has a mind of its own. It does not stay. One of the first lessons you will learn if you try to meditate for even five minutes is how unfocused your mind is. The unfocused nature of the human mind has been called monkey mind, because monkeys tend to climb and jump every which way. Like a monkey, your mind is bouncy, anticipating threats, and seeking out opportunities. The mind will see danger where there is none, and will try to cling to and increase pleasure when this moment is fine as it is. There is a reason for the mind's nature. Your mind evolved.

To survive, your ancestors constantly had to seek opportunities for food, shelter, and mates. Life on the planet you are riding on started in the oceans. Look at the little fishy on the next page. She is certainly enjoying the little plankton snacks, but she is already thinking, "What about when these run out? I must find more."

The craving, insatiable aspects of your monkey mind or fishy mind can ruin dinner or any pleasurable experience, by trying to cling to it, improve it, or compulsively jumping ahead in time to pursue even better meals in the future. Our fishy minds are even more reactive to dangers, both real and imagined, as the image on the next page demonstrates.

If any animal, including your ancestors were not ever-vigilant for dangerous and potentially lethal situations, and thus capable of instant action, then you would not be here. Your ancestors' genes would not have survived, and their genes would not be here in you now. Look at the two fish photos again, imagining your self in each of the two situations. The fear response is much stronger than the pleasure response.[7] If you miss one of those plankton snacks, you find another, or go a little hungry. If you miss the Megalodon behind you…

---

[7] The article *Bad is Stronger than Good* by Baumeister et al provides data from many fields that the brain perceives negative events more strongly than positive events.

So evolution created your mind as a survival device more than as a contentment device. We can still be happy, but we have a few challenges that often get in our way. Although the survival device explanation may seem a bit fatalistic and bleak, this explanation normalizes our anxiety and our self-focused and vigilant minds. Normalizing is a helpful step, because once you understand that your mind is normal in its vigilance and dis-ease, you no longer have to generate anxiety about your anxiety or criticize your self for having anxiety. You are an alert, vigilant, worried, and anxious person, and for good reason. You are a genetic winner in the brutal game called evolution because your ancestors were anxious enough to avoid predators.

Today there are fewer real predators, especially for those lucky enough to live in stable countries and neighborhoods. The stress-related predators such as cortisol, cellular inflammation, and the *Overs*, including over-eating and over-hating are far more likely to kill you than a shark or even a criminal who might want your wallet. The self-monitoring that was appropriate for life in the sea with Megalodons lurking in the shadows will also impede performance, as every new email from the boss evokes a potential Megalodon in the mind. Our best performances occur when we are not overly worried about outcomes or future threats and are fully engrossed in an activity, utilizing our creativity, letting flow happen. Understanding why our self is so worried and vigilant is an important step in changing our relationship to our self and our life.

5

Whoa Is Me

I've had many troubles in my life; some actually happened.

-paraphrase of Mark Twain

Despite the fact that having a vigilant monkey mind is somewhat natural, the jumpy self-focused qualities of our minds go too far and often make us miserable. Just because the mind evolved to be adaptive and functional, does not mean it is currently optimized or ideal. Much preventable human mental suffering could be placed under the broad categories of angst, dissatisfaction, craving, and self-criticism. We could also describe much of the suffering of the human mind as falling under the broad categories of anxiety and depression. By depression, we are including the full continuum, including any and all depressive and negative thoughts, even if the person does not have a depressive disorder. Anxiety and depression or mood disorders are the most common forms of mental disorders.[8] The vast majority of people who do not meet criteria for a disorder still know what it feels like to

---

[8] In a given year approximately 26% of people will have a mental disorder. The anxiety disorders are most common, followed by the mood disorders. In an effort to explain universal human suffering, we do not mean to deny that other problems such as learning disorders, eating disorders, schizophrenia, or bipolar exist. Nor are we minimizing the suffering that is often involved with those conditions. The severe mental disorders are real and can cause massive suffering. Yet it is also clear that anxious and depressive thoughts affect far more people than are affected by schizophrenia. This book is basically for the worried well and for the average human who wants to improve their mind and life.

suffer from too much worry, negative thoughts, and self-criticism.

Thus, in an effort to explore what is close to universal in the human mind and alleviate the most suffering possible, we are going to risk oversimplification by saying that most humans experience mental suffering, and that if we had to name that suffering, anxiety and depression or anxious and depressive thoughts would be a good starting point. Let us greatly simplify psychological anxiety and depression in terms of thoughts:

Anxiety: "Am I ok?"

Depression: "No. I am rubbish."

Anxiety =   worrying about...

Depression = condemnation of...   **ME**

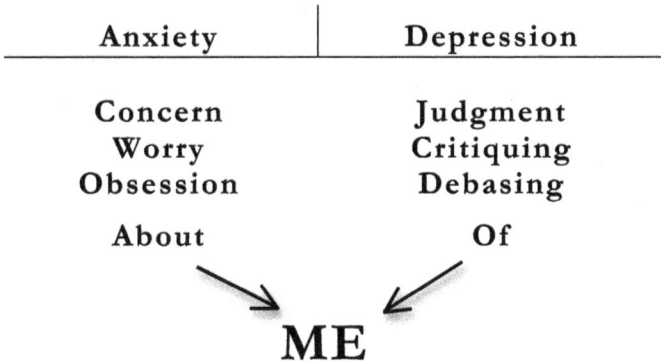

Anxiety	Depression
Concern	Judgment
Worry	Critiquing
Obsession	Debasing
About	Of

ME

Anxiety and depression and most of the related problems that go with them can be conceptualized as disorders of the self or self-consciousness.[9] This may seem somewhat obvious. My depression does not reside in someone else, the ether, or my leg. The observation that depression and anxiety are disorders of the self does not simply mean that the problems reside in the brain or in the mind. Pointing out that the self, self-absorption, and self-criticism are problematic means that certain styles of being, thinking, and believing, are less adaptive than others, and more likely to cause suffering. Anxiety and depression arise because of the mind's tendency to focus too much on the self as an object of awareness, worry, and criticism.

Anxiety is basically concern or worry in the form of self-focused thoughts, such as "How am I doing?" Anxiety likely evolved because we had to answer the life-saving question, "Am I in danger?" This type of anxious thinking certainly was adaptive or functional, can still be

---

[9] Although psychological conditions have strong genetic and biological contributions, we are bombarded with genetic and biological explanations because the science is newer and certain industries make no money from learning or experiential explanations, and thus have a stake in emphasizing that suffering is caused by neurochemical imbalances. The theory that all mental problems are caused by neurochemical imbalances has never been proven. It is as likely that when our mind experiences or feels suffering, our brain shifts its production, combinations, and delivery of neurotransmitters. It is also important to note that while biology and genetics play a significant role in mental suffering, depression is still *experienced* as an issue of the self. And if you want to address the psychological territory, you need psychological explanations and approaches. Please research and pursue genetic-biological and neuroscientific explanations and approaches. But within the realm of your experience, it is difficult to boost serotonin simply by talking about biological models of serotonin. You can boost serotonin by taking psychotropic drugs, eating healthy foods, exercising, petting a dog, hugging someone, or engaging in compassion practices. Dr. Weibel is not anti-medication and regularly refers to prescribers.

adaptive at times, but may be in need of an upgrade.[10]
Today you might get as anxious when a coworker looks at
you askance, as when the bear growled at the cave
entrance 50,000 years ago. Today many people remain in a
constant state of hyper-arousal, of small fight or flight
responses.

Just asking the question, "Am I ok? Am I ok? Am I
ok?..." is quite annoying. Everyone has likely experienced
their mind getting stuck in such a checking mode,
especially during high stress times, such as before a
deadline or during a life transition. Does constantly
monitoring how one is doing, actually advance how one is
doing? What percentage of your anxious thoughts helps
you? Or has your best work come when you transcended
self-consciousness and were immersed in a task?

Depression is typically not sadness about a tragedy,
such as genocide or a natural disaster in another country.
I may be deeply concerned and saddened by suffering
elsewhere, but I get depressed because the Dissatisfied
Self starts thinking "I am a failure." Sadness about
genocide is normal reactive sadness, perhaps normal grief.
Depression about the genocide would be more likely to
occur if saving the people of that nation is part of your
identity via a career in an aid organization, and then you
make critical evaluations about your self's performance
regarding that role, generalized these judgments to your
self as a whole, and conclude that your self is ineffective
and worthless. We can often bear others' suffering and be

---

[10] Physical evolution is slow. We still have tailbones. Cultural evolution, which
includes dancing, forms of government, and increases in tolerance can be much
faster. The current culture and all the progress that has been made provides the
backdrop in which any of us can evolve our consciousness within our lifetime,
which then will be a small influence on current and future culture.

supportive, but we worry and get depressed about our
selves.

Anxiety and depression, which frequently co-occur,
exacerbate and contribute to physical pain, and also lead
to escape behaviors such the Overs: over-eating, drinking,
drugging, exercising, dieting, sexing, gambling, shopping,
and risking. These attempts to escape anxious and
depressed mental states can lead to disasters such as
accidents, financial ruin, or wear our health down over
time.

Thus, the monkey mind's checking is too frequent and
nervous, and its judgments are often too harsh and
condemning. The self contains an inner critic who
reviews your every move with an obsessiveness that no
restaurant critic can match. It is as if we have an internal
drill instructor trying to whip us into shape, without
realizing that we would respond better to acceptance and
encouragement, or merely allowing us to be.

The self-conscious evaluations can also become
irrational. In the chart on the next page based on and
modified from cognitive therapy by Aaron Beck, we
reveal how irrational thoughts and beliefs almost always
focus on the self.

Irrational Self-Focused Thinking		
Catastrophizing	Disasters happen to...	Me
Overgeneralization	One instance labels	
Shoulds	Who should?	
Personalization	Everything reflects on...	Me
Mind-Reading	Who is a clairvoyant?	
Filtering	Who sees the negative?	Me
Blaming	They wronged whom?	
Paranoia	They are out to get...	

The most effective way to respond to the critic is not to bludgeon her, and move toward the opposite pole, bragging that your self is great. Positive self-talk and self-affirmations have some utility, but self-affirmations are limited and are not the most foundational or powerful method for arriving at relaxed, mindful, peak, or flow states. Compare the thoughts "I am great" or "I am confident" to your mindful, experiencing, or awe-filled moments. "I am great" certainly seems preferable to "I am miserable," but within the bragging we can see striving and seeds of insecurity. If you need to prop

yourself up with thoughts of "I am confident", you will
certainly remove that pedestal once your results change.

With affirmations, you are taking the extra effort and
time to think the thought "I am great.'" You doth brag
too much. Whichever God you believe in does not have
to frequently say, "I am great." Neither does a three-year
old enjoying the ocean for the first time. Neither does an
athlete performing in the zone.

Imagine you are about to putt to win the Masters or
take a penalty kick to win the World Cup. Self-
affirmations such as "I'm confident" or "can't miss",
target reminders such as "hole" or "net", or even victory
visualization words such as "champion," are not as
effective at inducing flow or in the zone performance as
are mindful approaches such as fully entering the body,
breathing, seeing without speaking, deeply concentrating
on the target with little need for word labels, and letting
the body's previous practice take over, letting the body
do what it knows how to do. Thus, self-chatter, and even
self-affirmations, are not the deepest or most reliable
path to wellness, peak performance, or expanding
compassion.

Potential Exceptions to the Dissatisfied Self

Pleasers

People pleasers appear to focus only on others. For
the majority of people with the pleasing tendency,
focusing on others is like a tennis tournament. They are
keenly aware of the score, even if they repress or deny
this awareness. The pleasers may focus outwardly on their
friends, families, or volunteer work, but they are deeply

worried about how these helping efforts reflect upon their selves. The pleasers are desperate to have others see them as concerned with others, and are terrified of being accused of focusing on the self. The pleasers are as self-focused as a person who is constantly checking their hair, but at least the pleasers do more social good. Let us give them that credit.

The pleasers often exhaust themselves and are not as effective at serving as they could be if they transcended the self, and helped in a more relaxed and flowing manner. We are not condemning these pleasers, but merely pointing out that what seems like an outward and serving focus, is often based on a need to impress others and esteem their self. We would like to keep the social good the pleasers do and maybe even enhance it, but help them relax and transcend the fear they have of their self-focused chatter which constantly says, "I need to please to be loved."

Haters

Haters direct hostility outward in the form of judgments and criticisms of people and the world. A person arguing against the Dissatisfied Self model might argue that these criticizers are not focusing obsessively on the self, but are merely noting actual problems in the world.

It is true that there are problems in the world, and that critical-thinking and criticism have their place (e.g., within science, product development, or politics). Look more deeply, however, and you will see that much criticism is self-criticism. At first this is hard to fathom and harder to accept. Your ego will say, "When I say the

world is awful, it is because it is awful." The key is to
notice that the objects being judged and criticized are the
people, objects, and conditions of my life. Outward
judgments are usually projected inward judgments. When
I am judging my job, my living situation, my spouse, or
my meal, notice the word that comes before the object
that I am judging.

"My job is absurd" can be translated as:

	good enough	
Why am I not	talented enough	to have a better job?
	smart enough	

The haters or complainers are almost always unhappy
with their selves. They are lacking power. The realization
that most criticism is self-criticism is simple yet deep.
When you realize this, you will start to notice that you
usually complain when you feel bad about your life and
your Dissatisfied Self is pulsating in the background. You
can also start to notice that the people who complain the
most are the most dissatisfied with their own lives and
are deflecting the brutality of their lurking *me*. You can
treat the complainer in you and others with more
compassion.

6

Your Head is a Brick

A tree that cannot bend will crack in the wind.

-Lao Tzu

Once the self starts forming, it forms quickly and rigidly. Having a self that knows your preferences certainly helps when choosing a vacation. However, quick and rigid adherence to one limited identity has drawbacks.

Let us examine how the identity forms. You want to survive, and love is the pathway. You have to convince the giant bipeds that you are worth feeding and keeping around. Luckily, Mother Nature provided babies with the cuteness advantage. Parents are also wired to help their genes survive and to love their babies.

But watch what happens out of parents' well-intentioned desire to love. At first they say, "She's so cute." There is not much else they can say. At six weeks, parents cannot really say that you are so smart. You are just a blob of cuteness. But eventually you start doing things. You elicit reactions in the form of ooing and cooing that you certainly can understand before you are fully verbal. Shaping begins.

Eventually, parents start labeling. "Look at Sally, she's my little soccer player," and you realize you now have a survival ticket. Whatever gets praised will be repeated. The baby you is like a captive dolphin who is shaped into jumping through hoops, using sardines. If left to their own devices, children are myriad; they are renaissance people. But you got praised for being an athlete, and decided, "I am an athlete."

Imagine if the first thing you did that got praised was somewhat random. Maybe Mom and Dad walked in when you had the soccer ball, but five minutes earlier you had a paintbrush, or vice versa. If you favor and develop one side of your self to win love, you may never develop other aspects or find your true nature. You become the first aspect of your self that was loved or the aspect that was loved most. The other dimensions of your self, other potential selves, wither on the vine from neglect.

Even worse than being boxed into one role, such as athlete, is accepting a negative identity. We also internalize negative judgments. Even good parents have grumpy moments. Children may also misinterpret neutral statements as criticism. Peers also might make negative comments. Thus, even if parents are exemplary, the child may hear from others or even decide on their own, "I can't draw" and believe it, and live it, rather than believing that everyone can draw, and they simply have not yet allowed themselves to draw. A child or adult might say, "I can't dance." Untrue. Every human can dance.[11] Dogs can dance.

Another and most pernicious form of shaping occurs because some parents should have their licenses revoked. If your unskilled parent said, "You are worthless," that parent still may have been your best source of love at that time.[12] Even if they were hitting you, they were probably providing some positives, even if minimal. They were hopefully still feeding you. So you may be willing to

---

[11] Some are even brave enough to do it without alcohol.

[12] Ending abuse of all types is a primary goal of an enlightened civilization.

maintain the consistent identity "I'm worthless" to keep getting fed. Most abused dogs get a chance to make a break for it, and many do not escape their abusers. Abuse is never pure abuse. It is intermixed with moments, even if brief, of love, of reinforcement, or at least of survival. Even if you are immersed in a concentration camp of a relationship, certain moments are pleasurable, such as seeing another day, breathing, or seeing a sunset. We can even come to love even our captors.[13] Because abusive love or abuse alternating with love is all you know, it may be preferable to the perceived alternative, non-existence or going out into the wild alone. To maintain the flow of love, no matter how intermittent and weak, the child performs a consistent identity show like a seal barking for fish.

Many of us stick with our given identities, just like our given names. We are stamped or branded early, and we accept it. We fear change, but what we really fear is losing love, jeopardizing our survival. We avoid loss more than we seek gain. We are risk averse. Some of us are so rigid that we will stick with mediocrity and misery, rather than risk change, because misery is comfortable and safe, or at least associated with survival. The self rigidifies.

Choosing an identity to win parents' love may have had some functionality when you were two feet tall, but solidifying the self is not the only choice once we have grown out of our maximally cute stage. You are now grown. You can rewrite your story, your identity, your self. You can move beyond me.

---

[13] See Stockholm syndrome based on a hostage situation in which hostages came to empathized and identify with their captors.

7

Shiny

For what shall it profit a man,
if he shall gain the whole world, and lose his own soul?

-Jesus

The self is a bling addict. Bling refers to light that reflects off shiny objects such as diamonds. Shiny is not bad in and of itself. Shiny can be beautiful, and appreciating beauty can be one method of transcending the self. But bling obsession is a harmful type of materialism. We will define materialism as a desire to boost the self, to increase the value of the self both in one's own mind, but more importantly in others' eyes by acquiring money, power, and possessions.

Materialism has not paid off. The scientific data from the field of positive psychology reveals that bling provides no lasting satisfaction. The research now solidly reveals that once you have met the basic needs including food and decent housing, which most readers of this book probably already have, then increasing your wealth will not raise your happiness. Pursuing more money than one needs for the basics will not raise your happiness.

Not only will chasing money not raise your happiness, materialistic values may decrease well-being, your sense of life satisfaction, and even your health. The data reveals that those with materialistic values show lesser well being, lower quality relationships, more antisocial attitudes, and have less concern over protecting the planet.

The time you spend chasing resources above the minimum required to achieve the basics, drains your ability to focus on quality relationships, creative outlets, or service to others, all of which have been shown to boost happiness. Humans want to be happy, yet we do the wrong things. It is difficult to think of an area of life where we are more misguided or where the stakes are higher.

As an analogy for misguided efforts, imagine a young man who wants to run a long distance, perhaps a marathon. This man decides to train by lifting heavy objects, perhaps rocks or small livestock, objects he can only lift four or five times. If he progresses carefully and systematically, he will get stronger and bigger, but he will not build the endurance to complete a marathon. The science on materialism appears to be as clear as the science of power versus endurance training. Bling obsession decreases happiness; a focus on relationships, creativity, and connectedness boosts happiness.

And yet we do the wrong things. Even when we know the research on materialism and happiness, it is still difficult to resist the pull of bling. Materialism is an escape activity; it feels good in the short-term, but so does heroin. Do your best to direct your efforts to activities that contribute to happiness, not fleeting highs. Do not be a marathoner who only lifts heavy rocks. Also have empathy for the people that do not know this research, or are not ready to hear it.

Notice how some people are constantly trying to enhance their self with shiny objects. The objects could be their body, possessions, or titles. Many of the magpies, the shine chasers, are wounded. Love their core, not their accoutrements.

8

Enter Alone - Leave Alone

Pray that your loneliness may spur you into finding
something to live for, great enough to die for.

-Dag Hammarskjold

It is an existential given that we enter and leave the world alone. No one accompanies us into our first light, and despite how many loved ones circle our dying bed, we exit alone. This does not mean that real connectedness in this life is not possible or important. The major task in this life is to use our freedom, and its implied responsibility, to make our own meaning in this lifetime before death. Meaning is usually realized via connections to others. Connectedness, often measured as social support, is also vital for health. Connectedness counters and can even outweigh the existential aloneness that is a part of life.

Despite the importance of connectedness to our well being, we often fail to achieve it, and more sadly, fail to try wisely. In *Loneliness*, John Cacioppo reveals data that people who are high in loneliness have higher stress hormones throughout their body. There has been a dramatic rise in loneliness in the past 30 years. In *Bowling Alone*, Robert Putnam explained that within the last 50-100 years there has been a dramatic decrease in community, social capital, and connectedness in the United States. Some of this is due to the changing society and demographics, such as people needing to relocate to pursue careers. Yet Putnam also reveals that technology intermixes with changing sociocultural norms, leading to "individualizing" of our leisure time via three hundred channels, streaming movies, video games, and virtual reality helmets. These technologies will allow us to choose our own adventure completely separate from others.

Social media may not be the answer. Like most things, social media can be both/and; it can connect and separate. The internet can promote movement toward a global tribe or global consciousness, such as allowing us to see first hand the destruction of wars and natural disasters in other parts of the world, and also to offer assistance. It is also true that social media is often not so social and not so connecting. Some studies show that hours using social media do not lead to more real relationships or feelings of connectedness, and actually contribute to depressive feelings, as we compare our everyday life to our online friends' highlights. It seems obvious that everyone puts their best face forward on social media. The people posting the most also tend to be higher in exhibitionism or narcissism.

In *The Culture of Narcissism* Christopher Lasch wrote, "Personal relations founded on reflected glory, on the need to admire and be admired, prove fleeting and insubstantial." The need for reflected glory may be increased or magnified by social media. If we compare our everyday life to hundreds of acquaintances' highlights, we may feel unfulfilled, envious, or sad in comparison.

Time spent on social media may not allow us to connect in real life, which determines whether such connections are good for our mood and health. People surf social media looking at long lost acquaintances' vacation shots rather than going to the local art opening, coffee house, or volunteer opportunity. Social media can promote connectedness if it allows people to facilitate connecting in real life. We can mindfully examine whether we feel more or less connected when using technologies. We can then compare whether looking at and using social media, walking the dog, visiting friends, volunteering, or other experiences leads to more connectedness.

The Luddites lost; we are not going back to writing on papyrus, nor will our kids give up texting or whatever comes next. Yet, we can bring awareness to our activities and mindfully spend more of our time in ways that help connect us.

9

No Joy in Me

I will be happy when I get...

a boyfriend
      a job
           a house
               married
                    kids
                         grandkids
                              retired
                                   dead

The Dissatisfied Self loves to judge the past and plan the future. It is afraid to experience the present because the present, and emotions, are unpredictable, like standing on a boat at sea. The Dissatisfied Self thinks the present is a waste of valuable planning time. The more dominant your Dissatisfied Self, the more of your day is spent worrying and planning. Time spent worrying or planning cannot be spent savoring. The more you focus on you, the more you miss.

Peak experience or flow states rarely happen when you focus on you. Researchers have studied people who were 'in the zone' or experiencing flow. Almost invariably, when asked what they were thinking during their flow moments, peak performers respond "nothing." Athletes who experience flow say something to the effect of, "My senses were totally aware. I could see clearly, but I wasn't thinking. I was doing. I was living." People recounting in the zone or flow experiences do not report having thoughts such as "I'm on fire" or "They can't stop me."

The athlete in flow is too immersed in the moment to remove themselves from the moment to comment upon it with a me thought.

If a person in the zone has anything resembling thought, these thoughts are simple, such as "Ball." Words are minimal and unnecessary. Flow is not verbal. It is experiential. It involves letting the body and its previous practice and abilities take over.

The same can be said about flow states in the arts. Artists report that creative bursts arrive when their mind is empty, not when they are brainstorming, forcing, or trying hard. The artists might be working long hours, but the creative burst does not feel like a struggle. There is little self-awareness. Artists relate the experience of the idea, song, or art coming through them as if they are a vessel or conduit for the art. Some have named this creative inspiration the muse, and they hope she visits frequently.

The muse or creative process is facilitated when we take a break from me, when we pause and mindfully attend. Once the creative flow state arrives, we are so immersed in experience that there is no space for me, as the creative process is so involving, tapping intuition and deeper levels of consciousness, that our self-conscious mind is quieted, allowing a state that is so enjoyable and rare, that we feel the muse is moving through us, utilizing us to deliver art to the world.

10

I Am Special

A man wrapped up in himself makes a very small bundle.

-Benjamin Franklin

Narcissism, defined as an inflated sense of self, appears to be increasing, particularly in younger generations in the United States. The Narcissistic Personality Inventory has been given out to college classes every year for thirty years, and narcissism is steadily going up among younger people. Jean Twenge presents data measuring the increases in narcissism and explains potential causes in *Generation Me* and *The Narcissism Epidemic*.

It is scary enough that narcissism is increasing, but it also appears empathy is decreasing. A meta-analysis of empathy studies found that self-reported empathy has declined since 1980, with an especially steep drop since 2000. This occurred in the same period that narcissism increased. It is not unexpected that increases in narcissism would coincide with decreases in empathy, but the confirmation of decreased empathy is particularly worrisome, as empathy is the basis for effective interpersonal relationships, from the workplace to our loved ones.

Twenge attributes the increase in narcissism to several factors. One was the well-intentioned but perhaps misguided self-esteem movement, which may have had some unintended consequences. The kind, caring, high-consciousness parents who came of age in the 1960's, and who witnessed or participated in historical and massively important gains in civil rights, wanted to give their children unconditional positive regard. This is certainly well-intentioned, and better than giving them lashes. However, it may be that the unintended consequences of unconditional praise for everyone has been a sense of entitlement and higher narcissism.

Another factor giving momentum to the self-esteem movement was several studies that indicated that self-esteem was correlated with higher academic achievement. Educators and policy makers made the classic correlation equals causation error and believed that self-esteem *caused* good grades, totally failing to grasp that the direction could be reversed, with achievement causing self-esteem, or that a third variable, such as intelligence, motivation, confidence, or even something unexpected such as good looks, could have been related to both self-esteem and achievement, and thus drive the correlation. The educators created a self-esteem curriculum to boost esteem, thinking it would boost achievement. Esteem boosting education included activities such as each child taking turns standing in the middle of their peers while the peers each say one thing they like about the child in the middle. This circle of praise sounds fabulous; please take us to a party with such a circle. On the other hand, real life, including jobs, rarely works this way.

Unfortunately, the point of the self-esteem circles in the classroom was to raise self-esteem, which would hopefully then raise academic achievement. Academic achievement did not go up. The movement to boost self-esteem took hold outside classrooms as well, and became part of the zeitgeist that continues today. The self-esteem movement is exemplified by practices such as not keeping score and trophies for every participant. Below is a song designed to boost children's self-esteem to the tune of Frère Jacques.

I am special, I am special (point to self)
If you look, you will see
Someone very special, someone very special,
It is me, it is me!! (Point to self)

Or this song to the tune of Twinkle Twinkle Little Star:

Special special special me
How I wonder what I'll be
In this big world I can be
Anything I want to be
Special special special me
How I wonder what I'll be

It is somewhat nice that these songs promote self-esteem and self-efficacy, but these songs lack a sense of connectedness, altruism, and esteem based on kindness or humility. Because the youth of today have been winning trophies for showing up, singing *I am special*, and watching reality TV participants achieve fame with little talent, a great number of today's young people think they are going to be famous. Twenge's research has revealed the percentage of young people who believe they will be famous, has dramatically increased in the last thirty years. The vast majority of the people expecting fame or riches are in for a rude awakening. Just because a miniscule percentage of people use the internet or reality TV as a springboard to being famous for being famous, does not mean that the odds of fame have realistically increased.

Multiply the frequency of a rare event, getting famous, and you still have a rare event.[14] Not only will today's youth not reach their exaggerated fame dreams, but they are facing ever-increasing economic competition. The fact that the average western young person today will not exceed the living standards of their parents, due mostly to global competition, is a first in history. One hundred years ago, the average person could reasonably expect to better their parents' material success. That trend continued in the United States until approximately the year 2000 when global competition, population growth, and a finite planet, made it apparent that people, especially Westerners, could not assume that they would exceed the living standards of their parents.

Twenge summarizes the wake up call of economic realities that awaits today's increasingly narcissistic youth with the phrase "Grandiose expectations, crushing realities." Higher narcissism will not buffer young people against tougher job markets, and will in fact make the fall from grace that much harder. One has to feel for these young people and for all of us. They went from getting a trophy for showing up to a new world economy in which a college degree no longer guarantees much. Besides making it harder to swallow the realities of the job market, narcissism makes it more difficult to connect.

---

[14] Assume new media has quadrupled the chances of becoming famous, raising the chance from .001 to .004. Your pragmatic chances of getting famous have not really changed even though it is 4 times or 400% more likely. At two decimal places, both probabilities round to zero. Getting famous was extremely unlikely both before and after new media made it four times easier.

The good news is that not everybody is a narcissist; there has simply been an upward trend in narcissism. There are still many empathic young people. And we must remember that many cultural trends are cyclical. Already there has been a major backlash against certain social media platforms, which now seem utilitarian, like a phone book or dictionary, rather than cool. We need to realize that fame or material gains never were the pathway to happiness. The U.S. economy and the average standard of living have tripled the past 50 years with no increase in happiness. Our materialism and the narcissism that is intertwined with it, have led the way in building unsustainable economies that threaten our existence.

The optimistic view is that more people, including young people, are now pursuing higher consciousness, which can lead to contentment that bling can never bring, and that this path is the same one that can help us maintain a livable planet. Part II will show us how to achieve happiness with no narcissism required.

11

Nothing Unites Us Like Them

If you go back in time you will find tribes that were essentially only concerned with their own tribal members.
If you were a member of another tribe,
you could be killed with impunity.

- Peter Singer

Us versus Them (UvT) is the tendency for humans to bond cohesively into groups and to have favorable biases for their ingroup and negative biases against the outgroup. We see the ingroup members as being more similar to us than they actually are, and as having desirable qualities such as charm, talent, or morality. We see the outgroup members as more different from us than they are, and as lacking desirable qualities and possessing negative qualities. UvT examples abound and include cliques, teams, and national rivalries. UvT thinking is powerful, often pleasurable, and potentially lethal.

We form groups easily. We need to belong. Recall your first day at a new school, moving to a new town, or joining a new organization. These situations can be exciting, but we desperately want to find a friend, an ally. We are social animals, and we require a tribe. If you have ever suffered a blow to one of your memberships, you realize how important a sense of belonging is. People define their selves by their groups, whether family, religion, or team.

Social psychologists have shown that it does not take much for us to form a group. The need to belong is so basic that we can invent a group as well as reasons why our group is important.

In a series of classic experiments Henri Tajfel and his colleagues found they could create a trivial commonality, and people would still form groups and develop biases against out-groups. Tafjel and colleagues flipped a coin to determine membership in two groups. The group members liked the members of their own group better and rated the members of their in-group as more likely to have pleasant personalities. Even though the group membership was as random as a coin flip, the participants immediately began favoring their own group. This type of research, called a minimal group paradigm, has been replicated and expanded. In some versions, people are randomly assigned to a group, but then have no opportunity to bond with or even see their group members, nor to see outgroup members. People will still favor their group, even if group assignment is random, and their group has had not time to meet, help each other, or compete against an outgroup. We can form an us quickly and with little evidence that we are different than them. If necessary, we invent the glue that binds us together.

Once we have a them, our us coheres. In the seminal Robbers Cave Experiment published in 1954, Sherif and colleagues split twenty-two fifth-grade boys into two groups to see how the groups would cohere, clash, and resolve conflict. All the boys were well adjusted, protestant, middle-class Caucasians from Oklahoma, who did not know each other prior to the experiment. The boys were matched on a variety of characteristics such as IQ to make the groups as similar as possible.

Sherif and his colleagues thought they would need several stages to create the conditions that would lead to conflict between the groups of boys, before they could then apply conflict resolution strategies. They were wrong. The between group conflict arose quite naturally and quickly. In the first few days of the experiment, when the groups were supposed to be separate and bonding within their own group, one group heard the other group on "their" baseball field. They considered this an intrusion, and expressed suspicions of the other group. The groups, which previously had not thought to name their groups, named themselves the Rattlers and the Eagles. The Rattlers put their flag on the baseball backstop, and made threatening remarks about what they would do if anybody bothered their flag. The Eagles attached their flag to a pole and said, "Our flag shall never touch the ground." The boys demanded to move to direct competition with the other group.

Before the contests began, one boy, Meyers, contemplated a peaceful strategy saying, "Maybe we could make friends with those guys and then somebody would not get mad and have any grudges." The next day, when the teams came into physical contact for the first time, Meyers changed his tune, calling one of the Rattler's "Dirty Shirt."[15] As the first baseball game began, the Rattlers sang "The first Eagle hit the deck, parley-voo. The second Eagle hit the deck, parley-voo. . ." Other insults hurled during the game included, "Little Black Sambo" and "You're not Eagles, You're pigeons!"

_____

[15] Use your imagination to modernize the insults. For some taunts, you will have to upgrade, possibly including foul language, while let us hope that "Little Black Sambo" would not often be heard at a modern little league game.

Both groups used religious ideas to bond and inspire confidence. After the first game, one Rattler prayed, "Dear Lord, we thank Thee for the food and for the cooks that cooked it, and for the ball game we won today." For the Eagles it became standard practice to huddle in prayer before games.

Each group developed a negative stereotype of them and a contrasting positive stereotype of us. Both groups minimized within group differences and maximized between group differences. After winning the 2nd baseball game the Eagles concluded that they had won because of their prayers, and the Rattlers had lost because they used cuss-words. The Eagles developed an image of themselves as proper-and-moral while the Rattlers decided they were rough-and-tough.

It is highly unlikely that all the foul-mouthed boys were assigned to one group and the clean-mouthed boys to the other group. It is more likely that the boys were looking for any way to distinguish themselves as different from the other group. One boy likely heard a boy on the other team curse and decided he could unite his team by saying "we are more moral than them." Imagine if the first boy had not heard the swear word from the other team, and five minutes later someone on his own team uttered a swear word that was overheard by the other team. It is likely that other team could have pigeon-holed his team as foul-mouthed, and that his team would have conformed to this label and begun cursing like sailors if it helped them bond together against those goody-goodys who were judging them. Groupishness arises quickly and develops momentum.

As the Robbers Cave experiment continued, the Eagles were disheartened after losing a tug of war. They were reinvigorated when they saw the Rattlers flag was still on top of the backstop. The Eagles seized the flag, set it aflame, and then re-hung the scorched remnants while singing *Taps*.

The Rattlers painted their arms and faces and raided the Eagles' cabin. They turned over beds, ripped mosquito netting, challenged the boys to come out and fight, and stole comic books and the leader's jeans. The next day they made a flag of the jeans after painting "The last of the Eagles" on each leg.

The next day the Eagles, armed with sticks and bats, launched a retaliatory raid on the Rattlers' cabin, turning over beds and scattering dirt. The Eagles returned to their cabin where they entrenched and prepared weapons, including socks filled with rocks, in case of a return raid. The phrase 'socks filled with rocks' or 'rocks in socks' is a frightening summary of the Robber's Cave experiment. The fact that 12-year-old boys, selected for their commonality, created potentially lethal weapons of socks filled with rocks after several days of summer camp competition seems to clearly demonstrate the power and danger of UvT.

The scheming, raids, and insults continued, until the researchers had to break up several fistfights. The researchers decided to end the competitive phase, realizing that the intergroup conflict was high enough and that the boys' safety may have been in jeopardy. The research camp then moved on to conflict resolution strategies.

The researchers found that contact without competition, such as attending a meal or watching movies together did not reduce friction. A shared meal turned into a food fight.

Conflict was reduced when the experimenters created a mutual problem requiring cooperation that allowed the groups to overcome their differences. The boys were told that vandals had damaged the pipes supplying the camp's main water tank. They were told to inspect the pipes and then meet at the water tank. The researchers had turned off the valve, placed large boulders over it, and stuffed a sack into the faucet near the valve. Both teams worked together to solve the problem and then took turns drinking water with no insults. Then the researchers told the boys that the food truck was stuck, requiring both groups to pull it free. When both groups were pulling in unison, the truck driver subtly hit the gas, with the boys believing they were the essential muscle. After this success there was much intermingling, and "backslapping."

On the bus ride home from the camp, at a refreshment stand, the Rattlers suggested that their winnings from the bean bag toss be used to buy milkshakes for all the boys. And when some of the boys at the front of the bus began singing *Oklahoma* all of the boys moved to the front of the bus and joined in the singing. The researchers reported, "The gaiety lasted during the last half hour of the trip; no one went back to the rear."

Robber's Cave is frightening because young humans with much in common were ready to rumble with rocks in socks within a few days of being divided into groups. Robber's Cave is also hopeful, however, in that the experiment shows that we can reduce conflict between groups when both groups realize they have a shared enemy or a mutual problem that requires cooperation.

Unfortunately, most of humanity does not yet perceive warfare between nations, starving children, or protection of the biosphere as mutual problems. The majority of humans do not yet appear to recognize that we share a home. It also does not appear that the space aliens are invading any time soon to bond earthlings into one tribe. Part II of this book will help us reach this one tribe mentality whether or not a hungry ET arrives to devour us.

12

I Am Savage

Red in tooth and claw

-Alfred Tennyson

Humans have always been violent. The first step toward transcending the bloodthirstiness is to admit it. An experiment with mice reveals how violence can be rewarding in the mammalian brain. In the experiment, one male and one female mouse are placed in a cage. The female mouse is removed and a male intruder is introduced. The first male mouse rattles his tail, takes an aggressive sideways stance, and boxes and bites the intruder. The researchers remove the intruder and train the first male mouse to nose-poke a target if he wants to let the male intruder back in the cage. The first male mouse consistently pokes the target to let the intruder in so he can box and bite again. The researchers then give the first male mouse a drug to block dopamine, a neurotransmitter associated with rewards in the brain, and the male mouse becomes less likely to poke to let his opponent back in the ring, hinting that the boxing and biting are motivating and linked to rewards in the brain. Essentially, when the buzz from fighting is blocked, the fighting ceases.

I once interviewed a Vietnam veteran and among many other questions asked, "How many fights have you had?" The veteran first said, "I don't recall" and after mild inquiry added, "too many too count." After a request for elaboration, the nonchalant veteran said that in the early 1970's in a rural setting, he would "go to the dance hall every week, walk to the middle of the dance floor, stand back-to-back, and take all comers." This ultimate male bonding experience seemed amazing and was followed up by questions such as "Did the police ever come?" The veteran's response, "They were there." It seems clear this this earnest and likable veteran had been getting a dopamine buzz like the mice. I got one just from hearing the story.

While the mice research and the back-to-back veteran describe the potentially rewarding feelings that can be associated with violence, the human capacity for violence clearly has a dark underbelly and history. With child abuse, sexual violence, murders, longstanding conflicts, civil wars, and genocides, there is little need to argue that humans can be violent. Besides the obvious costs of death and destruction, nations wasting time on war are draining their capacity to do other things, such as educating their populace or building sustainable economies.

Although violence might give some people a dopamine buzz, there are other ways to get such a buzz, such as cuddling a puppy. We must also look at the psychological reasons people engage in violence. Violence is most often linked with self-preservation and self-enhancement. Pecking orders are not just for roosters. You may need to fight to establish popularity, ranking, and power that the archaic or reptilian brain translates into the ability to date and mate. Women traditionally fought less with fists, but their struggles for popularity and mates are fairly well established. Many of our female ancestors also selected and mated with men skilled in violence. Nations fight for similar reasons, to protect their genes, resources, and future survival.

Besides competition for resources and mates, which seems somewhat rational, violence also emerges when our ego feels insulted or wronged, with or without actual danger to our body. We fight when the idea of the self is insulted. If someone insults something we are not identified with (e.g., a team in a sport we do not follow), we do not care. However, if someone insults something with which you are identified (e.g., gender, church, race, team), you react as if they insulted you, your body, your identity, your rights, your rank, or your survival. You might fight.

We often react to ego threats in the form of symbolic words (vocal sounds made by flapping lips) as if spears or blows are coming at us. You insult my ego (e.g., my favorite team), and I will defend my ego by risking my body, which is the real me (it contains my mind). From a mindbody perspective this makes little sense. My mind resides in my body. Why risk my body when the only thing threatened by a verbal insult is my Dissatisfied Self, a sub-component of my mind? We do not recognize that the symbols are not me because of over-identification.

Most people do not actually play on their favorite pro sports team, yet more than a few fights start because of vociferous sports rooting. Fights and riots start because people insult or even burn symbols, whether an athletic jersey, a flag, or black ink on paper, which can be easily replicated. We often pay no notice to the actual killing of humans, if we are not ego-identified with them, but an ego object, a book, is burned and some of us want to kill. Group violence is almost always due to the over-identification of individuals with a group. Personal ego transmogrifies into group ego.

The optimistic news is that the per capita prevalence
of violence is decreasing, which is a huge source of
optimism and evidence that we do have the potential to
culturally evolve. Stephen Pinker's *The Better Angels of Our
Nature: Why Violence has Declined* is a powerful review of
the evidence that most forms of violence are decreasing
whether we take a lens of 200 or 10,000 years back in
history.

The fact that human violence is decreasing is in
direct support of the premises of this book, that human
culture evolves, that each human can develop, and that we
are becoming a more empathic civilization, moving
toward a global village. Despite the great news about the
decreasing rate of violence, we obviously still have too
much violence and need violence to decrease more
broadly and faster. The new technologies of war also
mean that isolated psychopaths or terrorists can do far
more damage even if they are few in number.

Part II of this book will help us loosen the death grip
of the Dissatisfied Self on our lives. Hopefully, we can do
less damage this way, reducing the world's violence. We
also may have a bigger problem than violence. Even if we
end the wars between tribes, we already may have done
too much damage to our biosphere to allow humans to
thrive for another millennia.

13

It Might Be Over Soon

We abuse land because we see it as a commodity belonging to us. When we see land as a community to which we belong, we may begin to use it with love and respect.

-Aldo Leopold

We may have a bigger long-term problem than violence. All of us are doomed if we cannot maintain a livable planet. Environmental degradation and climate change are real. The biosphere may have already crossed several thresholds or tipping points, which may not be easily reversible and which could threaten all human life on this planet. The level of consensus about human induced climate change is rarely found in science. Climate change skeptics typically believe that an omnipotent power can push the reset button on the planet or have funding ties to political interest groups and big business.[16] Even if we are allergic to evidence and immune to science and find a way to deny climate change, we are still in trouble from all other forms of pollution and unsustainable consumption.

We are now experiencing the sixth extinction in the Earth's history, with the fifth being the one that we all know about because of the plastic dinosaurs we play with as children. In *The Sixth Extinction: An Unnatural History*, Elizabeth Kolbert summarizes scientific data and tours

---

[16] See Dunlap and McCright's *Organized Climate Change Denial* chapter in The Oxford Handbook of Climate Change and Society, or find their chart with a search for: Key Components of Climate Change Denial Machine.

the globe to visit habitats and the people who live there, to explain how the sixth extinction is happening now. The fifth extinction occurred 65 million years ago after an asteroid hit the Yucatan, creating a dust cloud that blocked the sun and doomed the dinosaurs. The sixth extinction refers to the current increase in the loss of plant and animal species. Estimates are that 20 to 50 percent of all species will be lost in this century. One study predicts no fish in the oceans by 2048. Many experts predict that by the end of this century there will be no more wild large animals: elephants, tigers, rhinos, or polar bears. Maybe in five hundred years they will become beloved toys, like current day dinosaurs, romanticized creatures from a long gone age. Humans likely can use technology to hang around longer than the bears and lions, but we still may be in trouble. Hopefully, the dying species will not die in vain and might serve as canaries in the coalmine, invoking enough fear to fuel wise corrective action among humans.

Please visit www.footprintnetwork.org, input data about your lifestyle, and an algorithm will determine how many Earths it would take to support your lifestyle if all humans lived like you. For the guilty fingers typing now, it would take the resources of 2.4 Earths to support us, the humans, at the author's current rate of consumption. He hopes to improve. For now, it seems we only have one planet. We might be doomed, not the Earth itself, but us.

Save the Planet is a well intentioned slogan, yet save the planet implies that we are heroes here to do the saving, and also forgets that the planet was here before us and will likely be here long after us or whatever we become via continued evolution. We need to save us and our descendants. The cockroaches will still be here.

Violence, poverty, disease, and environmental degradation are the biggest problems humans face that require the dedication and united efforts of the smartest people we have, as well as all of us making lifestyle changes. To facilitate wise and coordinated efforts, we also need to raise our consciousness. When consciousness changes, behaviors follow.

Many readers are likely old enough to remember a day when you actually had to convince the average person not to litter. Forty years ago, littering was treated as a prominent issue like today's attempts to end dependency on fossil fuels. Fifty years ago, a decent person might toss their trash out the car window on a country road. Being anti-litter was not yet established as an automatic belief and behavior in the average person's consciousness. Environmental agencies tried anti-litter campaigns telling people, "don't pollute", essentially trying to scold or shame them into behavior change. This rarely works. Ask your four-year-old. Behaviors flow much better if we believe in the reason for the behavior.

Then the anti-pollution activists focused their efforts on raising consciousness rather than chastising behaviors. The crying Native American commercial, which is not without controversy, was deemed one of the most effective public service announcements of all time. A Native American in traditional dress, was crying as he looked out at fields and streams filled with trash from city folk. Although today we might think of the commercial as politically incorrect and a bit sappy, in the 1970's many people thought it was sad, and they empathized with the Native American, who was saddened by the destroyed land. The commercial is an example of how empathic resonance can work better than scolding.

Some people still litter, but today it is fairly obvious to the average third grader that littering is wrong, unkind, and uncool. It is obvious because the average consciousness has expanded.

We certainly hope the readers of these words are already post-litter. Think about why you choose not to litter. It may just be a habit that your parents ingrained in you, but you also likely have empathy for the other people who live here. Once the empathy is there, the behavior is obvious. Ask any of your friends if they own slaves. Let us hope they do not. This is progress, the result of a sea change in consciousness. If you were alive two hundred years ago, a blip in terms of human evolution[17], chances are that if you were lucky enough to be born into the upper classes, you and a good portion of your friends would have owned slaves, as it was the norm, the water in which wealthier society swam. Many of the writers of our constitution and their peers had slaves. Now, the vast majority of sensible people are against slavery.[18]

Consciousness can change, sometimes quickly. Once it changes, compassionate behaviors are often obvious, not always easy, but obvious. The average level of

---

[17] Modern humans have been here for 200,000 years. $200/200,000 = .001$. So slavery went from acceptable among aristocrats and heads of state to deplorable, with most people believing it needs to end, in .1% of modern human evolutionary time. Promising. The mind, beliefs, and culture can change quicker than losing a tailbone.

[18] Slavery does continue, especially sex trade slavery. This is horrific and needs to be stopped. People nobly fighting the slavery trade say there are more slaves now than ever before. This is true, mainly because the world population is now 7 billion people, whereas in the year 1800 it was 1 billion people. Thus, there are more slaves now because there are 7 times more people. Slavery was practiced in the open by heads of state in 1800. Slavery is more rare per capita today. Huge progress has been made, and we still have a massive slavery problem that needs to be ended.

consciousness needs to expand if we are going to maintain a livable planet. It is doubtful that technology alone will save us. We are going to have to change our behaviors. We will likely have to tighten our belts to invest in new technologies that will not provide an immediate return. Reversing climate change is going to be difficult for many reasons including intertwined obstacles such as crushing poverty, income inequality, political turmoil, terrorism, and health epidemics.

All nations and most people in those nations are going to have to participate to slow and reverse climate change. It is easy to delay, blame, and pass the buck to other nations. Let us admit that it is far easier for some people to change and reduce emissions than others. Basically, the more you have in terms of money, education, resources, and consciousness, the more you can change. In his hierarchy of needs model, Maslow explained that we are motivated to meet basic needs before higher needs. The levels of needs are physiological, safety, belonging, esteem, self-actualization, and self-transcendence. We have to realize that it will be more difficult for some people and nations to change. The developing nations, outside of China, are not currently producing as much emissions as the United States but they are increasing emissions as they trying to increase their economies. Who can blame them? Many of the people on the planet are more concerned with finding shelter and their next meal rather than easing their conscience that the meal had a low carbon footprint.

Rather than drift into hopelessness, those of use who had the privilege of starting out with the first two or three levels (physiological, safety, belonging) met early in our lives, can use this privilege to try to reach the higher

levels of the pyramid. Those of us who were lucky enough
to have been born three rungs up, should treat it as our
opportunity and duty to try reach self-actualization, and
then possibly widen our empathy and perspective further
to transcend our selves and care for others, maybe even
everybody, including this place we live. Trickle down
economics has always been a questionable theory, but
trickle down compassion makes sense. Think of all the
times you grew more empathic. You likely grew in
empathy when you were loved, often by a parent, teacher,
or coach. Someone loved you and you grew in the
capacity to love. Ripples of compassion can have
profound effects as they reach outward.

We also should not blame people who were not
blessed to have their basic needs met.[19] An example of
blaming would be to say, "Why should the US clean up its
emissions, the developing world is not cleaning up their
act?" This is non-compassionate stance because it does
not realize that nations, economies, and people go

---

[19]Generalizing across groups and nations is tricky and risky. In certain academic
circles, you can be pilloried if you do. However, evidence (see the Progress section
of Recommended Readings) reveals that individuals, tribes, or nations, can develop
at different rates and have different challenges, beliefs, institutions, forms of
government, and average levels of consciousness. The well-intentioned idea of
pluralistic relativism often denies this by holding that the myriad forms of truth are
always partial and culturally embedded. Thus, we should not compare, let alone rank,
belief systems, behaviors, or cultures. Relativists often have a noble motivation to
avoid and rectify oppression such as occurred during colonialism. How dare a
westerner judge a culture by western standards? A decent point; let us be sensitive to
the lens with which we evaluate, and not be oppressive today. But relativism
handcuffs, as it does not allow us to fully describe and compare the realities of
oppression or progress. Pluralistic relativist, if you think all beliefs and practices and
culturally embedded, and different but equal in terms of morality, are you willing to
move your two young daughters to a region where people throw acid on girls for
seeking education? Some relativists have used culture to contextualize, explain away,
or even defend cannibalism and cliterectomies. Ouch.

through stages, and that it is harder to worry about saving the planet and transcending the self, when you have no food or shelter. When the United States was at the same stage of building an economy as a developing nation, we were clear cutting forests, strip-mining, and shooting buffalo from trains as sport.

Also, we must realize that the developing economies are trying to match our level of materialism and consumption. We have not exactly led by example in creating sustainable economies. Now we can lead by example, fully realize that materialism does not boost happiness and life satisfaction, and be world leaders in sensible, sustainable, and healthy communities, integrally tied to the global civilization. We can also invest in massive research efforts to lead the way in new technologies that will allow clean energy.

As an individual, you can use the opportunity you were given by having some of your basic needs met early. If you can even contemplate a level of consciousness beyond mere survival, beyond ego-focused drives, then you are indeed lucky. The world needs you. We need you, and as a paradoxical bonus, thinking and acting beyond me is the surest route to lasting meaning and life satisfaction.

It is everyone's responsibility, and we in the advanced economies set the bar of consumption that the developing nations are trying to copy. The first world readers with educations, grocery stores, and jobs could do more to raise their own consciousness, and then try to get governments to act as if they had a mid-level, if not high level, of consciousness. This book is not only about reaching enlightenment for me. It is about moving beyond me and then taking action to help others.

Conclusion to Part I

Just as the evolved tendency to be drawn toward sugary and fatty foods was once highly adaptive and now may actually be counter-productive, the self has useful functions but also hurts us when it becomes too vigilant and greedy. The overactive Dissatisfied Self is about as useful as an anchor on a boat. You certainly need one, but you also want your boat to be un-anchored at times, and be able to go fast and see the world. We need to move beyond the capabilities of the anchor.

The remainder of this book is about helping us move from egocentric to worldcentric, from a me-focus toward a consciousness that can be described as wider, higher, more compassionate, and more loving. The Compassion Practices in this book provide a method and a path to help us move up the slope toward higher consciousness. The path involves effort, risk, and some sacrifice.

Lifting the veil of ignorance created by egocentric thinking patterns will make you less likely to compulsively pursue hedonistic or materialistic pleasures. Being less compulsively hedonistic does not mean being less happy. If pleasures come your way, you will enjoy them more, as you will be present and content, but compulsive pleasures only for pleasure's sake will feel superficial and bland. You will not be as desperate to feed the insatiable craver within. You will not miss your compulsive escapes. Moving beyond me is the most reliable pathway to life satisfaction and deep contentment. It also enhances dancing.

A One.. A Two.....A One, Two, Three, Four.

II
Compassion
Practices

Introduction to the Dance

We have explored how a self is necessary, evolutionarily adaptive in many circumstances, and perhaps in need of an upgrade. Compassion is the salve or WD40 for the sticky mind-quirks that evolved to ensure our cooperation is rewarded and our share is not stolen, but which, when unskillfully engaged cause us to become toxic and dangerous. The Compassion Practices provide a path to widening our perspective beyond self-conscious concerns, thereby developing wider empathy, deeper compassion, and more joy. Most of the practices will be experiential, such as mindfulness and the cemetery meditation. Some will be thought provoking, such as exploring the limitations of your identity. The great news is that this process is not only about lessening angst and dis-ease. The same techniques that help us overcome self-focused angst are the ones that can increase feelings of connectedness and joy. Enough reading s y m b o l s on paper. Let us experience and play.

14

Mindfulness

Student: "How can I get myself to enlightenment?
Master: "Forget it."
Student: "I will never get there?"
Master: "Yes."
Student: "Darn."

The student leaves the monastery.

Master: "Why do these students keep leaving after I tell
them the way? I told her to forget her self, and there
is nowhere to go as she is already here. And she
leaves."

Our minds have a mind of their own. Imagine you
were setting out on a cross-country road trip, driving
from Brooklyn to San Francisco. You leave N.Y., and
against your will, your car drives straight north, to
Canada. This never happens. Our cars go where we steer
them. Our minds do not. Weird. Here we are supposedly
the most advanced species on this planet, and we are not
the captain of this ship, the driver of this bus. You might
intend that your mind focuses on a long-term goal today,
but your mind is often distracted and absorbed by
unbidden self-focused thinking: from neutral chatter,
"I'm hungry" to worry, "Is he the one?" to self-directives,
"I should be productive" to existential terror, "Will I
achieve my dreams?" or self-condemnation, "I am a
loser." Mindfulness begins with recognition of the nature

of the mind, and then shifts the game by changing the way we relate to thoughts, the mind, and the self.

Mindfulness is paying attention to the present moment in an accepting way. An easy and foundational method of practicing mindfulness is bringing awareness to an object of awareness in the present, the most common being the breath. You can develop the ability to return attention to anything in the present, whether the breath, hearing, seeing, other bodily sensations, or emotions.

Mindfulness is simple, difficult, and powerful. How can M[20] be both simple and difficult? Welcome to paradox, the nature of the universe. M is simple because children do it naturally before they get covered in layer after layer of egoic concerns. We have all been mindful. During the best moments of our lives, we were fully present.

M can be difficult because our minds are naturally checking for threats and seeking resources. If you engage on a quest to be more mindful, you will likely have to remind your bouncing monkey mind to be mindful 263 times per day for the rest of your life. A charming Nepalese student in one of my classes did a mindfulness exercise and then observed his mind thusly, "It seems like jumping fox trying to get grapes."[21] Exactly.

We also live in mindless times. We must process endless information and make hundreds of choices per day. Our current brains, evolved for a simpler and more brutal environment, and have not adjusted to an environment in which too many bear claws are more likely

---

[20] The word is not the thing. Hence *M* can point to mindfulness, and requires less key strokes.

[21] Rabin was a Nepalese exchange student. I found his writing, including the less than perfect English, to be amazing. He gave permission to use his quotes.

to kill us than any bear outside the cave. The environment 100,000 years ago was certainly brutal in terms of life expectancy, but it was likely easier in terms of information to process and decisions to make. A daily decision in the past might have been to hunt or fish, and your choice of mate would be from among ten same age-range people. Your time frame would be to get enough food for the next winter, not to plan a retirement thirty years from today. Life was brutal, but the amount of information you had to process each day was less. Today, every email can be perceived as a threat and advertisements frequently remind us what we should crave to make us complete.

Despite the above challenges, M is powerful because it is the most reliable way to step outside the battle of self-focused worry and criticism. M changes our relationship to our thoughts and our self. When we are mindless, we go with thoughts. We buy into thoughts; we become thoughts. We have angry thoughts - we are angry - we are overcome with anger. The red mist has descended. Once we have practiced M for a while, just noticing thoughts and returning to the moment with awareness, we will gain an ability to pause, an objectivity, and a space that changes our relationship to our thoughts and to our self.

The mindless sequence:

"They wronged me intentionally."

↘

"I am angry."

↘

ANGER

Transforms into:

"My mind is currently generating angry thoughts."

or

"Mind is generating angry thoughts."

or

"Angry thoughts arising."

You step back from being overpowered by negative thoughts and emotions to witnessing that you are not your thoughts. Your mind has thoughts, but they are not you. "I am not my thoughts." This is a massive discovery. It is one of the reasons that M practice has been called insight meditation.

Once we gain some detachment from the thinking mind, we will slowly be able to take all self-focused mental reactions less seriously. We will spend more time noticing that lived and felt experiences are more real and more important than interpretations. We will know that the ever-present self-reflective commentary does not help us experience, and is non-essential for achieving, creating, or being.

M will help you the take idea of *me* less seriously. Rather than believing that there is an ego, a self behind your eyes, driving the show, you will appreciate that you are an organism, a collection of sensations that can have experiences, but the experiences do not all need to be experienced from the first person, as if you are the only character. If it is raining, you do not need to think, "I am witnessing rain. How does this rain affect me? Do I like it?" It is just raining. Wet. Just now.

We have gained a tiny glimpse into the insight *'There is no self.'* It can take years to truly grasp this, and you do not have to fully grasp it to benefit from M practice. For starters just realize that there is no permanent, rigid self, who is the owner or driver of your life. Show us your self from yesterday? Or tomorrow? Place it in your hand. We see your body, and we know there is a brain in your skull. But we do not see an ego, a self. We see an organism that has not danced enough lately. M helps the dancer within get beyond me so the music moves them unimpeded by ego censorship.

Mindfulness

Enjoy practice. Here is a basic recipe to help you begin.

1. Observe your mind (sensations, thoughts, emotions) with acceptance.

2. Notice...

    Is your mind experiencing the present?

    If not...

3. Bring your mind back to the present and experience it fully.

4. Repeat steps 1-3 forever.

You may want to listen to a teacher in person, if possible, or an audio track when you practice mindfulness. Jon Kabat-Zinn has many audio tracks available, as do other teachers whose books are in the Recommended section of this book. Tracks with my voice and script are available at beyondme.life or drweibel.com. One good point to remember is that the body is always here, so M often focuses on the senses and sensations in the body. You can be mindful of any part of the body. Your breathing is a great object or process of awareness to focus on, as it is always present and it is already happening. Walking meditation focuses on the process of moving and placing the feet on the ground. Yoga is mindful movement that can liberate your mind while shaping a functional and resilient body. Any experience or sensation that is here in the present can be your anchor, your method of practicing mindfulness. The purpose is the same, to immerse fully in the moment, bypassing the self-absorbed thinking mind.

You can use M now to relax, to give your mind a rest, or to make better choices. M can help us feel our emotions and learn from them, without being dominated by them. When you drop out of constant self-chatter, you drop into experience, and you often realize peacefulness and equanimity.

M is also the primary and most reliable path to self-transcendence. In many ways this entire book could be about M. Every practice in this book will be better if done mindfully. M is perhaps the most dependable tool that can help us realize the silliness of over-attachment to our ego stories, while simultaneously helping us to engage more fully in every moment of life. M is the most tried and true technique used by regular folks and contemplatives to move toward higher levels of consciousness.

There are many books on mindfulness, but in reality, these books are all pointing to the moon and yet not the moon. They are the map and not the thing. They are slightly different descriptions of the same techniques and experiences, just as this book is. Read a book, possibly this one, or one from the recommended readings, then set the book down and practice.

Easy Pause

Some people say they do not have time to meditate. This excuse does not hold for exercise nor for meditation. Regarding physical exercise, the no time excuse does not fly because exercise makes your brain and body more efficient. If you are in the most stressful period of your life, whether studying for final exams or working full-

time while parenting three kids, you do not have time to
not exercise. If you squeeze in time for an intense twenty
minutes of exercise, your brain will be 30% more efficient
for the next six hours and your body will have more
energy the next day.

With meditation, we get similar gains in terms of
calmness and wisdom. Do you have time to breathe? We
thinks so. To meditate, you merely need to let go of your
other concerns and observe your breathing for a few
minutes. The Easy Pause or three-breath-meditation gives
us a reachable goal of paying attention for about one
minute. Simply attend to your breathing for three breaths,
using the gentle labels to help you focus and deepen the
experience.

Easy Pause

In, Out
Deep, Slow
Connect, Embrace

The Easy Pause can be a vacation in your otherwise
hectic day. Attend to the inbreath and outbreath while
silently saying the label. On the 2nd breath, you might
notice that your breath will be slowing without conscious
effort by the time you say "Slow." The third phrase is
customizable. Use your creativity. "Connect, embrace"
signifies connect to the moment and embrace the world.
You could use Here, Now; Peace, Presence; Here, Home;
or One, Love. Invent more phrases. Easy Pause will wet
your appetite for longer mindfulness sessions. Eventually
you might try a multi-day retreat.

Although M requires continual choices to return to the present, M practice does not have to be a struggle. You reap benefits every time you return, as M practice is the path to experiencing simple pleasures, living with joy, and opening to wisdom.

15

Loosen Up

Blessed are the hearts that can bend; they shall never be broken.

-Albert Camus

The drive to find and maintain one's identity begins in early childhood, is strong during adolescence, and in reality never stops. While a child needs to establish an identity, contemplatives of all traditions have pointed out that rigid attachment to a self-contrived view of a permanent self is limiting. Buddhist psychology has gone so far as to propose that 'there is no I' or 'there is no self', meaning we are an ever-evolving conglomeration of processes, intimately linked to everything around us, and that we change in every moment. To challenge your view that you are you, a solid, permanent entity, contemplatives might ask simple yet profound questions such as "Where is the thing you call a self. Show me your self? Can you hold it in your hand? I see a body continually changing." Trying to answer these questions, you would have great difficulty producing a self, as we really are a collection of bodily and cognitive processes, not a stagnant entity.

Thus, we can redefine ourselves in any moment, and there is no need to become overly attached to ideas or labels about our selves, about who we are or could be.

Shake Those Labels

Please write twenty combined answers to the phrases:

"I am a _____ [insert noun]."

or

"I am _____ [insert adjective]."

You will likely have a great deal of pride in many of these descriptions of your self. These labels are part of you, a source of memories, and may have bonded you to the people you love.

Yet, for this exercise let us open our minds and explore whether any of these labels separate us from others or limit our options. Go back to the list of labels and write down if each label separates you from anyone, or limits your experience in any way. For example, could pride in your tribe ever be a barrier to connectedness? Does being a fan of one team prohibit you from dating a fan of your team's most bitter rival? Could being strongly identified with one gender ever limit your empathy for the other? If you envision your self as wild and adventurous, do you ever separate your self from people you think of as uptight or strait-laced?

Open your mind to the possibility that a strong and fixed identity could be both stabilizing and limiting. Identities exclude. Or they certainly can if one clings to them too tightly. Experiment with loosening your labels and your self.

16

Reclamation

Every child is an artist.
The problem is how to remain an artist once we grow up.
-Pablo Picasso

When we are young, we shape our selves to win our parents love and survive. Imagine being left outside as a baby or toddler by your caregivers either in present day or 5,000 years ago. In either period the result would likely not be pleasant. In ancient times there were more bears, and today there are more cars. Conveniently, at first we are just blobs of beauty to set our parents' hearts aflutter so they are more likely to care for us and less likely to walk down to the corner bar.

When we finally start doing things besides look cute, parents will shape our behaviors with their compliments. The mythical ideal parents, who want to give unconditional love and support to whatever is in the child's heart, will still shape the child by complimenting and encouraging the first actions they see. In a survival strategy, you, the child, will likely repeat whatever is praised.

What if your unconditional parent walked out of the room while you grabbed a paintbrush, but walked back in when you grabbed a soccer ball? Or vice versa? Thus, the mythological parent can still undermine the child's true nature by praising too quickly and strongly and not allowing the child to explore myriad potential passions naturally over their lifetime.

What if our parents read the unconditional love books, but cannot live up to this ideal? Despite our best intentions of not over-shaping our children, we are more likely to notice when the child engages in things we like, and probably will show more enthusiasm. Other parents may be more overt in their shaping, "My boy is a warrior" and "Look at my princess." You will be happy if your child does your favorite thing, and likely ecstatic if they exceed you. This non-jealous love involving vicarious achievement sounds great, yet how much more pressure is placed on the child when we as parents, both consciously and unconsciously, wish that our child exceeds us? Is hoping that my child exceeds me that far from needing my child to exceed me? Although this love is non-jealous, in that we want their success, it carries pressure.

Thus far, we have talked about competent parents who succeed at delivering unconditional love to different extents. There are also plenty of troubled parents, who likely were not loved well themselves, who dole criticism or inconsistent love, or who model or even praise reckless or violent behaviors. Children of these parents are going to be confused, and will settle on an identity that promotes love and survival. Like a low plant in the rainforest, these children will grow at any angle, however distorted their shape, contorting themselves to reach the faint rays of light.

Regardless of the type of parenting, the child will bend their self to win love. The ball starts rolling, and the child settles into a role, a personality, and a self that they believe will win the most love. While the parts of us we think will win love may grow, other parts may wither on the vine.

Reclaim Lost Parts

Ponder what you may have given up on the path to becoming who you are. Did you shed any creativity, sensitivity, toughness, assertiveness, athleticism, laziness, aggressiveness, playfulness, seriousness, or other attributes? If you gave up any of these, or if they were never allowed to fully develop, can you experiment with letting any of these dimensions back into your life? It is never too late to be that painter or athlete. Relish the beginner's mind. Embrace reasonable standards and the potential for progress that comes without forcing. If you ride a bike around the block, you are being athletic.

Beware of any limiting, all or none, and generalizing thoughts such as "I'm not athletic" or "I can't draw" You may have internalized the voices of your parents, coaches, and peers. Witness these voices as you try something new, and never let them stop you. Your parents and teachers had their own limits that you can transcend in your own life. At some point we have to become our own parents. In no way does this invalidate or disrespect their contribution. In fact, it may give us more respect for the efforts they gave to parent us. Love your parents, have compassion for their limitations, and transcend those limits.

You can reframe limiting thoughts to "I haven't yet developed my _____ abilities." or "I have not experimented much with dancing." It is almost an impossibility to say you cannot dance. If a paralyzed person can blink her eyes to music, she is dancing.

17

Cemetery Stroll

> We are all going to die, all of us, what a circus!
> That alone should make us love each other but it doesn't.
> We are terrorized and flattened by trivialities,
> we are eaten up by nothing.
>
>   - Charles Bukowski

Many spiritual traditions have emphasized the contemplation of impermanence as a method for overcoming self-absorption and finding meaning. Contemplating impermanence can give us perspective, a sense of connectedness, and greater compassion.

The Buddhists were perhaps the most ardent explorers of impermanence. Certain Buddhist sects have a tradition of meditating for days at the charnel grounds, sites along rivers where bodies were cremated or left to decompose. While this is a good example of impermanence practice, there are other methods of contemplating impermanence that are perhaps more accessible.

Symbols of impermanence that we can contemplate include the hourglass, each grain passing from top to bottom representing a week, day, or moment in our ever-shrinking supply. We also can use the lens of science, pondering the second law of thermodynamics, the principle of entropy, which dictates that energy always dissipates. Examples of entropy include the fact that every animal dies and that a leaf on the ground is no longer a leaf after several months. No energy is lost, but the leaf loses its leafness; its energy has dispersed into other forms.

The Buddhists have a lovely concept of 'already broken.' Everything, including all living things, our bodies, and our possessions are (in terms of cosmic time) heading toward dust and are thus 'already broken'. It is not as easy to get upset about a scratch on your car when you realize the car was 'already broken', subject to the laws of entropy, or at least heading toward an owner other than you. Think of all the cars you have owned. How important to you are the scratches on the cars you no longer own?

Impermanence promotes peace of mind and forgiveness. Imagine someone does not return one of your books. Remind your self that the book was already broken; soon its pages will be decaying. We also can use this principle to handle insults, whether insults to our abilities or bodily insults in the form of a creaky knee, with more equanimity, realizing our bodies are already broken. Realize that the self could benefit from being more broken or more flexible, as word based insults can only touch a self that is defended, rigid, and afraid.

Impermanence is liberating. When you realize your problems are small and temporary, you are free to enjoy what is. When you understand that the grains of sand are rapidly crossing the waist of the hourglass, you seize and appreciate each one.

Pondering impermanence, especially pondering death directly, may sound scary. You may be worried that too much pondering of death might induce hopelessness or a sense of desperation. In a paradoxical twist, for the majority of people, contemplating impermanence fosters reverence for each moment, rather than fostering desperation that our moments are finite. We fear death in inverse proportion to how well we have lived. When we consider death soon enough and often enough, we may live well enough to not dread death's arrival.

Desperation emerges when we ponder the end of our ego, contrasting what we have achieved with our ego's grandiose expectations. Impermanence helps us realize that everyone who came before us was impermanent, and everyone who comes after us will be impermanent. Impermanence helps you step outside the ego and see its desperate grasping with clear eyes. You then can choose to play a different game.

Striving and bragging lose their allure with the perspective of an impermanent existence. Imagine that near the end of your life, you think, "Wow, I have exceeded all my expectations. I am stupendous." This type of thinking would be narcissistic navel gazing, which would not help you smell the roses in your remaining moments. This type of thinking is not the door to contentment. Happy people are immersed in the now, not obsessed with their trophy collections. This space rock we are sitting on, and all life on it are impermanent. Let us transcend the self-focus, attachments, and strivings, and drop into this body, this breath, and this beautiful moment.

Cemetery Stroll

Visit a cemetery and ponder impermanence. Spend time sitting or walking mindfully. If the cemetery is old, you will notice old headstones, possibly from many generations ago. You might realize a sense of connectedness to previous generations. If it is your hometown, you can realize that although human structures have changed, the land, the water, and the views are basically the same as they were when earlier generations lived.

Think of the people here as role models. They loved, played, and struggled until their journey was done, just as we will. You are not the first one to have problems. Ponder how no one visits many of these graves. It may seem sad, but it can be liberating, as you realize your daily troubles really are small. Imagine taking a survey of these people and asking them how they would relate to their old worries.

You might notice details such as differences in the markers, from a simple mossy stone in the grass to a thirty-foot marble pillar or a huge two-ton granite orb. You might ponder what type of symbol you will want when your time is over. You may notice that in earlier eras women's tombstones read 'wife of' as the primary identifier. Society advances; progress happens.

Realize that you too will soon be dust. This helps us see that we are all in this game together. Nobody gets out alive. Rather than make us sad, the cemetery stroll can connect us to previous generations, free our selves from trifling worries, and sharpen our focus on living a meaningful life.

18

Dice Games

Don't be too timid and squeamish about your actions.
All life is an experiment.
The more experiments you make the better.

- Ralph Waldo Emerson

Luke Rhinehardt's *The Dice Man*, a fictional cult classic novel, helps us realize that having one rigid, uni-dimensional identity, or true self, is as fun as racing a sailboat with its anchor down. The formation of the 'true self' begins early. The best parents try to give unconditional positive regard and praise their child early and often. The child enjoys and needs the parents' love and protection and will repeat whatever was praised. And so it begins. "That's my Sarah, she's a champion."; "Aaw, Johnny, he's so sweet."

This is not so terrible, but the other potential selves wither and shrink. The identity develops momentum and becomes solidified. Society and our peers also reward and enforce stability. Once your friends know you are the 'sweet' or 'tough' one, they want you to stay that way in their minds, and in your behaviors. They place you in a category and lock you there, to automate their own processing, so they can move on with life's complexities. They will filter evidence and will even create situations to confirm your identity.

Once you are trapped in a uni-dimensional self, it becomes comfortable. Because true flexibility is not valued, we become afraid to change, even when it would help us. Many people choose to stay in certain misery

rather than embrace the changes that would loosen the
ground beneath them, leading to temporary uncertainty
and chaos before they would reach a new equilibrium.

Rhinehardt's character, the Dice Man, says

> "to accept one self as the 'true' self implies that
> thousands of minority selves will die a slow death
> from neglect. Dozens of aspects of the person
> will never see the light of day. This is one reason
> we experience boredom and conflict. We refuse
> to recognize that a minority impulse is a
> potential full person, and that until that self is
> granted the same opportunity for development as
> the 'true' self, our personalities will be divided
> and susceptible to periodic explosions and riots.
> Psychology tries to solve conflicts by urging
> people to suppress their natural multiplicity and
> build a single dominant self to control the selves.
> This totalitarian solution means that an army of
> energy must be maintained to crush the minority
> selves' efforts to see the light of day. The
> average or normal personality exists in a
> continual insurrection."

The search for a singular self may also be a relic from
the societies from which we evolved. Robert Jay Lifton's
book, *The Protean Self*, describes why we now need a
shape-shifting self in an era in which the rate of change
continuously increases. For the vast majority of human
history people lived in tribes of approximately one-
hundred people. In this tribe, you would have one
primary identity, such as fisherperson or basket weaver.
In this type of stable society a narrow uni-dimensional
personality would suffice.

Currently, the speed of change, quantity of information, and diversity of choice are ever increasing. In a rapidly changing and multivalent society, the diverse, flexible, or protean personality is more adaptable, healthy, and enjoyable. Uncertainty, change, and even chaos are the nature of the universe, and selves that can embrace this will thrive.

The Dice Man may be the ultimate Protean human. He used the die as a tool to loosen the personality and free the many potential selves. He would place behavioral options on the dice and give over control to the dice. By doing this, the potential selves that had withered in the service of the true self were allowed to breathe the light of day. Dozens of potential selves whether the artist, singer, daredevil, or safety-conscious person were liberated. Rigidity faded in the face of the dice. Although *The Dice Man* was fiction, the theory and techniques have much in common with behavioral experiments as well as exposure to fears that are central components of evidence-based behavioral psychotherapies.

A common critique of dice games is that the dice roller still makes the choices. True, but the roller can be creative. Let your friends make the choices. Decide you will act like the next person on TV. Decide to go talk to any of six people in a room. Your creativity, common sense, and the rule of law are the only limits.

Dice Games, which can be called random living, will help you gain freedom and lessen the effort you spend repressing your selves. You will become a shape shifter, capable of multiple roles and more adept at thriving in an ever-changing environment. You will also have fun.

Roll the Dice

Dice games encourage flexibility of the collection of changing processes we call a self. Many people feel limited in the way they do things. Even wild people may not be able to embrace flexibility by being calm or obeying laws. With dice games we break out of our normal identities by giving self-control over to the dice.

Let the dice decide what route you take, what you eat, or where you go on vacation. Let the dice decide whether to begin dancing. At a party, assign each of six people to a side of the die, and then go hug whomever's number is rolled.[22] People whose primary self is reckless can experiment with timid, safe, and law-abiding selves. People who are rigid can let the die set them free in myriad ways.

1. Get a die or two dice, and decide that you are going to hand over control of your 'self' to the dice.

2. Choose behavioral options for sides of the dice, or choose two options for an even or odd roll. Ensure some of the options are challenging, forcing you to step beyond the carapace you call a self. Tight people will be challenged by adventurous options while the risk takers will be challenged by quiet, rule-abiding options.

3. Roll & embrace flexibility.

---

[22] Do not break laws or be unkind when playing. This practice is for compassion, not recklessness. Loosen up, even when following instructions to loosen.

19

Consider the Opposite

Out beyond ideas of wrongdoing and rightdoing
there is a field. I'll meet you there.

-Rumi

Usually, we attend to the world in ways that support
our existing beliefs, petrifying our identities into ever
more biased confirmations of our previous beliefs.
Converging evidence in fields such as cognitive
psychology, behavioral economics, and neuroscience is
revealing that we are not quite as rational or impartial as
we believe, and that much of our reasoning, including our
prosecution of contrary positions and promotion of
favorable positions, takes place outside of our awareness.
We see evidence that supports our beliefs, and filter out
evidence that is contrary to our beliefs. Once you learn of
an idea you like, you start seeing it more frequently. You
can live thirty years, and not know about an artist, and
then hear about and like her, and start seeing her work
everywhere. Frequently, we see what we like and confirm
what we already believe.

We tune in when we hear our views and change the
mental channel when we hear opposing views. We are less
likely to see counter-evidence, and if we do see it, we
refute it before it crosses the moat of our defenses. We
hate being wrong. If contrary evidence somehow gets
through the filter, we have an ever-ready supply of
weapons to defeat positions that are opposite our own.
Metaphorically, our brain possesses an ever-ready internal

litigator with a tenacious disposition, whose job it is to
make us think we are right and our opponents are wrong.

Ponder for a moment that you, yes, the fortress of
beliefs u[23] call u, may be susceptible to bias and
irrationality. If you are brave enough to let this idea gain
a foot in the door of your mind, your ego will most
certainly defend itself. Your ego might say, "Well I admit
I do not know everything, but I know much about the
fields which are my passions, my areas of expertise."
Surely, you do take in much information about your
passions, but you are also highly identified with them,
and thus even more likely to process data about your
passions in a biased way.

Regarding your passion, being wrong is too
threatening to your identity, and your mind will not let
you be wrong. The dissonance would be too great. Hence,
you are biased. Have you ever watched someone totally
identified with a topic, be challenged with a persuasive
argument they have not yet pondered? Do they
immediately change their views? The average person does
not even hear the evidence. Or they almost blow a gasket
rushing in with their best-prepared defenses. Our biases
lead us to paint the person with new views as 'other', and
then to demonize them. Recall, the Robber's Cave
experiment described in Chapter 11 about the social
dynamics of us versus them. Teenage boys, selected for
their sameness, and divided into two groups, invented
insults and a mythology to demonize the others and were
filling socks with rocks after five days of tug of war and

---

[23] Do misspellings upset u? It is only print or pixels. The symbol u is not different
than the third symbol in you. It is not a lion chasing you, a boss firing you, or
someone slandering you. It is a symbol. Try not to be a pilkunnussija.

baseball. Reviews of the evidence for human bias are provided in the recommended readings. Here, let us try the experiential approach by singing the Bias Song.

The Bias Song

I am right,
and you are wrong.
Come join me
and sing this song.
Evidence will surely be found.
Enemies belong in the ground.
Those who oppose are sick in the head.
So naïve they are better off dead.

This song is intentionally extreme and ridiculous. It is a dark joke. Yet is it completely unrealistic? Are the attitudes portrayed in this song five times more extreme than those attitudes that are prevalent in strongly partisan groups existing today. If you are reading this book, you are likely not as biased and hateful as these groups. Yet, you can likely recognize the tendencies in the Bias Song. This song is just a bit more extreme than the chants between bitter sports rivalries.[24]

Pointing out the wrongness in *them* feels self-justifying and self-enhancing. What if you did not need to attach your ego to your existing monolith of beliefs? What if you could trust in the moment, the process, and endless learning rather than clinging to one mountain of beliefs?

---

[24] Find the Manchester United football chant, "In your Liverpool slums." In doing this research, we realized Chelsea also has a version.

Consider the Opposite

Chew on a chunk of humility, and accept that you are often wrong. The best science says so. So if you want to be correct about the most current brain science, admit you are often irrational, biased, and wrong. Although this may sting a bit, it can also be liberating. It can be relaxing to say "I do not know", to assume a beginner's mind, and to be open to new ideas.

Consider the opposite point of view from one of your strongly held beliefs. Charged political issues might be a good area to consider. Or choose something smaller, such as a household debate (e.g., wash the dishes immediately or allow a pile to form). Notice what happens when you first bring to mind a view or belief that is directly opposed to yours. For example, as soon as you hear someone talk about political views that are the opposite of yours, your defenses rise, and you prepare for battle. You even get a tiny shot of adrenalin, about 1/5 of what you get before an athletic contest, yet still noticeable. This battle-preparedness is a small fight or flight reaction, and in this state you are less open to receiving information and learning.

There are certainly views that are or were opposite ours, that might have benefitted us now or in the past. Yet, we likely did not hear them. We can also consider views of ours that are now different than our past views. Which of our selves, past or present, was correct? Which was more moral?

Immerse yourself in the other opinion. Take on the beliefs of the other point of view. Do not do this in a satirical way, as some comedians do, parodying or mocking the other side. Rather, try to understand how the other side came to reach this conclusion. Walk in the other's shoes. Sit in the other position, so that you could somewhat sincerely argue from that position. Actually hold the beliefs until you feel that the belief has some validity. It does for the other. Trying to believe these new beliefs may feel fake, like an actor's first rehearsal of a part, but do it anyway. Actors rarely feel their characters at first. Do not fear that this one experiment is going to convert you to those beliefs. The edifice of your beliefs is too firmly entrenched. Your self is too strong. You are going to have work the practices in this book for a while to loosen the ossified you. Try to see slivers of validity in the other beliefs, and gain a fragment of understanding for those who hold them.

20

Radical Acceptance

There, but for the grace of God, go I.
- John Bradford

Radical Acceptance is another way to understand the other's views, thus expanding empathy and broadening consciousness. One use of the term radical acceptance means total acceptance of the moment and everything occurring within it. Often the most difficult part of mindfulness is that the mind wants to evaluate, judge, and change the moment. Radical acceptance reminds us to stay, dig in, and open to what is.

Another use of the term radical acceptance refers to how we can accept another person, even enemies. If your nemesis stands before you, how do you fully accept them? You might try to stay mindful, but your emotions might overwhelm you, causing you to want to lambaste the person. Radical acceptance of another means exactly what it sounds like, accepting fully, wholly, all aspects of the other.

We are going to call our enemy 'a person with whom my mind has difficulties' to acknowledge our responsibility, that our minds may contribute to the judgment of the other person's 'badness', rather than assuming that the other's badness is an objective truth.[25] When considering our enemies, the people with whom our

---

[25] There have been bad people such as Hitler and present day psychopaths. Nevertheless, much preventable human suffering is caused by our labeling others as bad based on our own biases and projections.

minds have difficulties, we often do not understand how they came to be the way they are.

Scientists, scholars, and many lay people believe that the sum of any person is nature plus nurture, genetics plus experience. All we are is genetics plus experience. If I had your genetics and experiences, I would be you. This premise is simple and powerful. Try arguing against it.

Now you have the answer for how the person with whom your mind has difficulties got to be who they are, how they got to hold those beliefs. They are the product of genes and experience. No more. No less. If you had their genes and experience you would be them. Consider that genetics and experience are somewhat of a crapshoot. You did not choose your genes, parenting, siblings, town or nation of birth, neighborhood, early schools, or peers. This radical acceptance exercise may help us realize a commonality with the other as we see that we are similar to them. We are both products of our genes and experiences. We may also see, "I could have been the other."[26]

The phrase, 'There but for the Grace of God, Go I'[27] is one that describes and can support the practice of radical acceptance. It is much easier to accept the other when I realize I could be the other.

---

[26] John Rawls' *A Theory of Justice* proposes a method for thinking about morality, indicating that we could build a society as if we do not know who we would be in this society. In this hypothetical society, I would not be me; I might be born of a different class, gender, color, lower IQ, with abusive parents, and no prospects for education. Behind this "veil of ignorance", we might make more empathic and moral decisions, really sitting in the shoes of those who were born less fortunate, and also realizing our privilege.

[27] The phrase has been attributed to John Bradford, but there is considerable debate about its origins. He actually said, "There but for the grace of God, goes John Bradford" but the popular version is now a saying attributable to him.

Radical Acceptance

Please consider a person with whom your mind has difficulties, someone who your mind has labeled "enemy" or "ignorant."

Realize:

If I had your genetics and experiences, I would be you.

Ponder this. Imagine sitting in the other's body and mind for a moment. This does not mean that your mind and soul would be in their body. You would be them. Your mind would be their mind. You would not have your beliefs, abilities, or intelligences. You would have theirs.

If previously you were blessed with a high IQ and parents who encouraged and paid for education, you now might be in the cranium of someone you previously called "ignorant", who was born with a below average IQ, and who was forced to stop their education due to poverty, family chaos, or violence. You are no longer you. You are them. Now jump back to your existence. Are you any slower to condemn the other?

You could have been them. I could be you; you could be me. If you sit with this exercise enough, you will realize that at subtle and not so subtle levels, "you are them." We are all connected. When they suffer, you suffer, eventually. I am you. You are me.

21

Naikan

Humility is not thinking less of oneself,
but thinking of oneself less.

– C.S. Lewis

Naikan is a 500-year-old practice designed to increase interdependence, gratitude, and humility. Humans have a strong tendency to attribute our successes to talent or hard work and our failures to external factors, such as bad luck. We reverse this interpretation for the successes and failures of others. For me success is talent while failure is bad luck. For others, their success is luck, and their failure is a lack of talent. This interpretive tendency is so prominent in humans that it has been called the Fundamental Attribution Error.[28]

Naikan helps us develop gratitude and humility by contemplating that we are not the only factor responsible for our successes. The first part of Naikan involves recalling all the people, institutions, and systems that have helped us and then developing feelings of gratitude for them. The second part of Naikan involves considering all those people who we have burdened in any way. In Japan, people will go to a Naikan center where they practice alone for three days, living with a mat, paper walls, three meals, and their own minds. Most readers of this book will not be in Japan, so we are going to recommend 20-minute sessions that can be repeated as often as you wish.

---

[28] *Thinking, Fast and Slow* by Daniel Kahneman is a seminal review of the science of cognitive psychology, including forms of bias.

Naikan helps us remember that our lives (our successes and failures, and in fact all events) are not only about us, nor were they caused exclusively by us. Humans, and particularly Westerners, often emphasize intense and almost total individualism in the form of statements such as 'I'm self-made.' Accepting responsibility certainly has benefits, and is essential for change. On the other hand, when we overemphasize the self at the expense of a more connected worldview, we misperceive reality and create burdensome pressure on our selves. In the Naikan exercise, we question the idea that we are totally self-made by pondering all the people, resources, and systems involved in creating the person we are at this moment.

Some people may have a resistance to practicing Naikan. They may believe that they will lose their self-esteem and confidence if they do not remind themselves that they are self-made. This fear is unwarranted. Rather than lower our self-esteem, Naikan boosts gratitude and helps us realize how far we have come, how many people supported us and are with us.

It is lonely being on an island. If you are entirely self-made, you and only you bear the responsibility to ensure that you stay at your current level. Naikan helps us realize that we are not alone; we stand on the shoulders of hundreds of people that have helped us. Our foundation is solid. Our roots go deep. The deep gratitude that results from Naikan practice can help us build wisdom and ease that feels more rooted and grounded than any confidence due to affirming how great I am.

Naikan I

Please find a comfortable place to sit or lie down for twenty minutes. Deeply consider some of the following questions in an effort to develop gratitude for all the institutions and people who contributed to who you are now. You may also let your mind create its own questions and drift into its own form of gratitude. Aim for feelings rather than intellectual analysis. The questions are mere pointers.

In what era were you born? Did you have to run on bare feet chasing huge beasts with a spear to get a meal? Was it a war torn region or a peaceful state? Were you born poor, forced to work at a young age to help the family have enough to eat? Had previous generations struggled to build society to the point at which you entered it? Were there principles of democracy and human rights in place? Did you have parents and receive love? Did you have access to health care? How many people were involved in helping each of your teachers acquire their knowledge so they could teach you? Did you play sports? Who invented that sport, bought the balls, volunteered to coach you, or built the fields? Did you get to listen to or play music? Did you have role models? Think of the thousands of people and institutions involved in producing everything in your life, from your shoes to your most cherished hobby.

Are you really self-made?

Or are you a connected, integral part of a holistic system that has been supported and nourished by people and systems both past and present?

Naikan II

Consider all the people who you have troubled in any way. The intent of this exercise is not to make you feel guilty, but to develop humility and gratitude. Think of all the people who may have been burdened or annoyed because you exist. Your parents may have changed your diapers out of love. There may have been many occasions when changing the diaper was a joy. Also admit that there were many times when your parents were tired and were not thrilled to deal with your waste. Your parents would have been happier if you were waste-free, or they may have preferred to sleep through the night. We bring joy, and we burden.

Naikan encourages us to be specific about exactly how much or how frequently we may have troubled the world. For example, you might think "Thank you parents, grandparents, and day care providers, for changing my diapers 4562 times (5/day x 365 days/year x 2.5 years)." The point is not math, but to realize the magnitude of the sacrifice of those who supported us.

How much time, effort, and money went into feeding you for the first eighteen years of your life? In many other ways we burdened teachers, coaches, and many others who care for us. We are not denying that these people may have gotten joy from serving us. We are just admitting that they also may have struggled; they may have had hard days, and we were a part of their burden.

There may be instances in which we troubled people more directly. All of us have been pouty, bratty, and manipulative, while others of us have done physical or emotional damage to others. We are going to recall that we are not perfect.

Naikan may seem that it is designed to instill or magnify feelings of guilt. But it really is designed to help us feel less entitled, less righteously indignant. For example, if we get cut off on the freeway, we instinctively think, "How dare they? How could they be so incompetent or inconsiderate?" In that moment, we are fueled by an affront to our ego. We are thinking we are justified, and we have forgotten our past transgressions. If, however, we have embraced the practice of Naikan, we realize that we have made dozens of intentional and unintentional mistakes, in which we burdened or even hurt others. This makes it much easier to forgive the driver who we believe has made an attack on us.

Naikan rebalances the scales of what we owe versus what we are owed in favor of gratitude. When we spend three days, or many twenty-minute sessions, considering that the world changed our diapers thousands of times, and granted us tens of thousands of other favors, while we created thousands of troubles for the world, we are essentially many thousands ahead in terms of fairness or gratitude events. So the infraction by the other driver lowers our advantage by one. We are still thousands ahead in the economy of gratitude, and might let the driver's infraction slide, sparing the driver and our body from our hostility.

In Naikan we are not beating ourselves up; we are recognizing that we are part of a holistic system, and that every part of the system takes energy from and gives energy to the system. This understanding will lead to enhanced gratitude and greater cooperation with our fellow travelers.

22

Forgive

Teacher: Have you forgiven your captors?

Student: No.

Teacher: Then they still have you imprisoned.

-unknown[29]

Forgiveness has long been a goal and practice of the world's spiritual traditions. Modern research on the benefits of forgiveness has grown rapidly. Forgiveness research has shown that people can learn to forgive, and that forgiving leads to health benefits.

People often resist the practice of forgiveness because they believe the transgression was wrong and the behavior does not deserve to be forgiven. Whenever we introduce forgiveness practice, we need to explain that forgiveness does not mean condoning or even forgiving specific behaviors or offenses. You can keep your belief that the behavior was wrong. You can protect yourself, enforce a corrective action such as a prison sentence, or choose to never see the person again. This is a little different than the typical lay usage of forgiveness. In lay usage, if a wife forgives a husband, the implication or assumption is that they will make amends, that all will be forgiven, including the behavior. Within this chapter, it almost seems as if the forgiveness practice could be renamed *Understanding and Letting Go*. We understand the context surrounding the situation and let go of hate that

---

[29] Found in Jack Kornfield's *The Art of Forgiveness, Lovingkindness, and Peace.*

eats us alive. However, *Understanding and Letting Go* might be too broad and vague as it could mean understanding almost anything, and it loses some of the focus that there was a perceived wrong. We will keep the term forgiveness; just keep in mind that we do not have to forgive a behavior, and we will be doing a great deal of understanding and letting go of hate. Forgiveness is also primarily for the forgiver. It is about letting go of anger, the endless quest for rectification, and the thirst for vengeance.

Both the ancient wisdom traditions and the modern forgiveness treatments emphasize that it is the stories we tell our selves about wrongs done to our selves, or the grievance story that keeps people's rage alive and prevents them from forgiving. The grievance story is the story you tell your self or others about how you were wronged. Grievance stories have unique qualities that you will begin to notice once you listen. The aggrieved person argues in an animated style, presenting evidence that they are just and righteous, and that the other was morally wrong. People sound like prosecuting attorneys while promoting their grievance stories. Try offering a different perspective to one of your friend's grievance stories and prepare to be added to the list of transgressors, or to duck. Many people become obsessed with their grievance story, and the case against the offender can actually grow with time, even when no new offenses occur. If the aggrieved person's life takes a turn for the worse after the offender has left town, the aggrieved may add the new tragedies to the list of original offenses by the transgressor.

A grievance story and a grudge are almost synonymous, but it is more precise to say the grievance story contains the details that feed the grudge, a strong fixed belief in the other's wrongness fueled by angry emotions. Holding a grudge with the vice-grip of self-righteous indignation is such a powerful state that we do not notice the grudge; we are the grudge. The grudge engulfs us; there is nothing else, no room for awareness. There is only the other's wrongness. The first time we notice what the grudge is doing to our mind and body, we will likely be shocked. The grievance story and the accompanying grudge keep us stuck, bound by our indignation like a ship in dry dock.

Many grudge-holders are possessed with a thirst for vengeance, even if the there is little chance for real retribution. Even if the transgressor is no longer living, a grudge holder might tell the world of the deceased offender's deeds, attempting to sully the offender's reputation among the living, or possibly even trying to deny access to heaven by reminding God of their sins. Our finite energies can be put to better uses.

Why is it so hard to forgive? Like most mental systems or behaviors, a lack of forgiveness and a thirst for vengeance evolved. For most of human history we lived in tribes of approximately one-hundred people. If a neighbor did not return your fishing nets, or a friend tried to seduce your wife, you had better watch out for these guys, as they lived three huts away. The tight quarters in which we evolved made it important for us to watch out for free loaders, to remember transgressions so they would not be repeated, and to guard our reputation so others would not think of violating us. The emotional pain driving a lack of forgiveness seals a transgression in memory and motivates us to punish the offender and restore our reputation as someone who will not be victimized.

Today, living in much larger tribes, we are not required to see many of our transgressors again, unless we keep them alive in our grievance stories. It is true that some transgressors are the people very close to us. However, it is still helpful to understand that a lack of forgiveness and even the thirst for vengeance are emotions that evolved in an earlier time, and that these evolved modules or programs in our brains may be losing a bit of their functionality.

It is also true that offenses or transgressions exist on a continuum of severity, and that the more severe offenses are going to be more difficult to forgive. Whether to forgive is a personal choice, but we need to make an informed choice about whether we want to free our mind from anger and vengeance. We also need to realize that people get stuck in plenty of grievances that an objective observer would not find egregious, and that the lack of forgiveness hurts the grudge holder more the transgressor.

An obstacle to forgiveness is that people cling to their vendettas and their misery. This is counter-intuitive, but people do seem to prefer certain misery to uncertainty. How could this be? In many instances, we try to lessen our pain. If you have a wood sliver in your finger, you pull it out. You do not like the discomfort. More precisely, your body does not like the sliver, as it generates pain, so you use your brain (part of your body) to direct your fingers to remove the painful sliver from your body. Fairly simple, but compare the sliver to ego-based misery.

The misery that people cling to is ego misery. It is pain associated with the ego, with my identity. Pain does not become ego misery until I say, "I have..." or "I suffer from..." Then the ego can cling. The ego likes feeling real, permanent, and important, and it does not care if it does it via grandiosity ("I am great") or via misery ("I am in so much pain because of ..."). Either way the ego gets what it wants, continued existence and attention from our awareness. If my ego were able to attach to "I have sliveritis, a condition based on having a sliver in my finger," your ego might unconsciously influence you to leave the sliver in the finger or at least to bemoan how much you suffer from the sliver.[30]

The ego is often scared and vulnerable. The obsession with the grievance and the quest for vengeance allow the ego to remain front and center, to feel big and important. Once you understand this counterintuitive point that people can cling to pain, you will begin noticing many examples.

When someone with ego-associated pain hears about a potential solution, they often say, "no, that won't work." It is true that they may have had many frustrating encounters while seeking remedies, including misdiagnoses, and perhaps a lack of compassion. Still, some people seem inflexible about possible solutions. If

---

[30] In *The Power of Now* Eckhart Tolle explains the counter-intuitive idea that the ego accepts and even accentuates pain to make itself, the ego, bigger. The idea that part of me likes pain is a hard one to swallow. In no way does this concept of the ego clinging to pain deny that physical and psychological pain exist. If you break your leg, it will hurt. We are simply noticing that all pain is felt by the mind, that we are not always masters of our minds, and that the tricky little ego can exacerbate the situation.

you hint that there could be a method to relieve some of their pain, they get defensive.[31] Listen to how much energy they put into statements such as "I have _____" or "I am a _____ sufferer" and see if you can hear the ego asserting itself. Remember the ego does not care if the person is miserable; it wants to be front and center.

People with ego driven pain will sometimes start arguing for their pain that they supposedly want removed. The make a case for their pain. They start saying, "It's real. I have it. I have tried everything." They are implying, "I will always have it." This is odd. Yet, when we notice the tendency to cling to grievance stories, vengeance quests, and pain, we are empowered. We see why it is difficult to forgive, but we are now motivated to release our grudges.

---

[31] Please do not start telling your friends that their conditions are ego-based. The point is for you to transcend your own ego and then go serve. The good news is that the best way to help a friend who may have ego-based pain is to love and support them as if they had pain due to a broken leg. Loving them allows their ego to be less fearful, which hopefully helps it feel less need to create drama and pain.

Forgive

We are going to expand our perspective to develop a fuller understanding of and even empathy for our transgressor or at least the conditions that led our transgressor to be how they are and act like they did. Your mind may initially resist the concept of empathy for the offender. If empathy is too difficult, think of the term understanding. Try to open your mind long enough to do this practice.

Begin by noticing other people's grievance stories. Our own grievance stories are so personal, so entangled in the structural beams of our self, that we cannot objectively hear, let alone question the grievance stories. Practice listening to others with a keen ear and empathy. Notice how the grievance teller's voice, body, and face change when they tell the story. Is the grievance story a commentary on where they have been and how far they have come, or is it a commentary designed to excoriate the violator, while the collateral damage remains the grievance teller?

Ask yourself whether you feel closer to or more attracted to the person while they tell their grievance. You might appreciate that they were willing to share an intimate story with you, but their anger likely pushes you away or at least makes you feel less close. An exception would be if you both have a grievance against the same transgressor. Now you are grievance allies, joined in bitterness. If your friend's grievance story is not against one of your nemeses, you likely will want to change the topic once they launch their prosecution.

The cruel irony is that the person needs empathy, but the anger and tension aroused by their telling of their grievance story pushes others away. Emotional contagion means that I feel your anger in my body; it is uncomfortable. A person with many grievance stories is bitter. Bitterness is rarely attractive.

Once you have some skill at noticing grievance stories, choose one of your own to release.

1.   Choose one of your grievance stories.

Choose a grievance story that is stuck, does not serve you, and that you are ready to release. Start with a mild offense, one that falls below five on a 1-10 thirst for vengeance scale.

2.   Retell the story and notice what happens to your body.

Imagine a good friend sitting with you, and you launch the story. Start making your case. Get into it. Once you are in it, take a few mindful breaths and notice what is happening to your body. You will most assuredly notice muscular tension. You will likely notice your blood pumping faster. You will likely be ready for a fight. But where is your opponent? Does your heart feel good when it is full of animosity?

3. Accept responsibility that you retell the story, keeping the feelings of anger alive.

A transgressor may have violently wronged you, but you retell the story. The offender is responsible for their actions. You are responsible for retelling your story.

Every time we retell our grievance stories, we make our selves agitated and unhealthy.

Estimate how many times you have told your story. Each time does not have to have been the full story. If something jogs your memory, making you say, "that jerk", your mind can summarize the story in an instant; it has rage shortcuts.

4. Decide I am tired of retelling the story

Buddha said, "Holding on to anger is like grasping a hot coal with the intent of throwing it at someone else; you are the one getting burned." Deciding to release the anger does not mean I am forgiving the behavior or indicating the transgressor deserves to walk free if they are currently serving time. Deciding to practice forgiveness means I want to clear more space in my heart-mind for positive emotions.

5. Re-write the story

A. Accept that truth is relative, memory is imperfect, and
    narratives evolve.

Both philosophy and cognitive science provide evidence that truth is relative, meaning that it is very difficult for a human mind to perceive and understand absolute truth. By saying that truth is relative, we are not saying your experience is false. If you were the victim of any type of violence, that is what happened. You have deep empathy for your suffering and pure disapproval for the act. At the same time we can realize that many people hold on to grievances that are far less wicked.

We will practice both/and thinking and admit that some horrific offenses happen, and also that offenses vary widely. For the smaller offenses, it is easier to appreciate that human memory is imperfect, humans are biased, and ego is ever striving for size, even if pain is the required ingredient. The events in the grievance story are from your viewpoint. Other storytellers and witnesses to the story will have different viewpoints. This is obvious with lesser grievances such as housemate disputes or romantic squabbles.

B.   Embrace a narrative approach.

The narrative approach indicates that stories and characters within stories can evolve. The importance of the story is how we think about it. The truth of the story is in us, and the story is free to change. Imagine an old-timer who witnessed the birth of jazz in Harlem, and his partner has noticed that the stories about the glory days have only gotten grander with each decade of his life. Is the old-timer lying? Or can narratives change. When the story changes, we change. At one level it is true that you cannot change the past. However, you can change your stories of the past.

C. Loosen the rigidity with questions

Is it possible that I misperceived any of the events? Is it possible that I misunderstood the offender's actions? Their intentions?

Intention is the difference between murder and manslaughter. Intention matters to all but the most extreme behaviorist. If I intend to hurt your feelings, I might be a psychopath. If I did not mean to hurt you, I am a fellow member of the species, perhaps stumbling as I maneuver through the minefields of the infinitely complex social milieu.

Explore whether there were any hidden intentions in your grievance story which you did not fully grasp or may have misunderstood. Is it possible that the person saw things differently? Is it possible that an objective witness may have seen the situation differently? Is it possible there was a variable in the story of which you were not aware?

D. Imagine what it was like to be your offender.

Sit or lie down, relax, and visualize what it was like to be your transgressor. Take your time and get into the role. You must do it sincerely, not using the exercise to build a further case against the offender, fortifying your grievance story.

In *Five Steps to Forgiveness: The Art and Science of Forgiving*, Everett Worthington had to practice the forgiveness he had preached as both a Christian pastor and a psychology professor who had researched forgiveness for years. After he had already dedicated his life to forgiveness scholarship, two teenagers broke into his mother's house and killed her during a robbery. In the book Worthington does an amazing visualization, in which he imagines himself as the culprits who killed his mother. He does it fully and with great detail, imagining the difficult upbringing, economic conditions, lack of education, desperation, fear, and adrenaline that influenced his mother's killers. Using imagery, he walked in their shoes. He imagined how the robbers almost assuredly wanted the house to be empty, and how they were likely terrified when they realized someone was home. He experienced how they likely panicked, and killed her in moment's notice. The description in his book is an amazing illustration of doing forgiveness work. He actually felt what it was like to be the boys who killed his mother. He realized that no one who does horrific deeds is feeling well.[32]

Worthington did not excuse or forgive the behavior. He understood and pitied the killers. His rage dissipated. His thirst for vengeance waned. His compassion greatly expanded, giving him the ability to hold both his beloved mother and her murderers in his understanding. He has love for one and pity for the other, but both are now within his field of compassion.

6. Find new meanings

This is your chance to re-write the end of the story, the epilogue that may continue to this day. Victor Frankl survived the German concentration camps, witnessing hundreds of murders as well as deaths due to disease and starvation. He certainly could have succumbed to PTSD and a lifelong quest for vengeance. Instead he invented logotherapy, a psychotherapy based on the importance of meaning in each person's life. Frankl found that those

---

[32] Scientists might raise an objection that psychopaths can enjoy hurting others. However, it can be argued that the psychopaths did not receive a good hand in the genetic deal. How would you like to be born with low empathy? While you might be spared feeling the suffering of others, you stand little chance of connecting with them. Thus, we can actually have empathy for those who have none. It is also true that the vast majority of psychopaths also receive poor nurturing.

who could create a sense of meaning were more likely to survive the concentration camps. The meaning was personal and individualized; it could be helping other members of the camp or surviving the camp to play the piano again. Frankl found that meaning provided life satisfaction as well as served as a buffer against even the most brutal stressors. Nietzche's quote, "He who has a why to live can bear almost any how," touches the core theme of logotherapy. Frankl's work and logotherapy continue to inspire millions to engage life and open to the meaning in their lives. If something horrific happened to you such as losing a limb in combat, you could return to teach others how to play adaptive sports. Your new meanings and the efforts they inspire can be in the open or behind the scenes. Flexibility is encouraged. You are the author. If you received a brain injury due to reckless driving, you can encourage teens to be careful in a way that no non-brain injured person can. Write your ending. Write your story.

23

Walk Lightly

Treat the earth well,
It was not given to you by your parents,
It was loaned to you by your children.

-Native American Proverb

"Walk lightly on the earth" is a Native American blessing and expression with broad implications for choices, lifestyle, and morality. Walking lightly or softly involves being quiet, respectful, and doing the least damage possible. Walking lightly involves realizing that just by being here, I am a user, a consumer, and in small ways a destroyer. Good deeds I do may counteract the resources I use and the destruction I do, but I still can cultivate the awareness that being alive means using up resources. It means creating waste.

Walking lightly involves having reverence for the earth. Most people would not walk on their children or symbols of their God because they care deeply about these things. It is interesting that we often literally and metaphorically stomp on our only home, the planet.

Walk Lightly

Step 1

Go to www.footprintnetwork.org to determine how many Earths it would take to support your current lifestyle. Contemplate whether you can cut down on your footprint.

Step 2

Go to a peaceful place and ponder how heavy is your foot and its print? You can consider issues such as: all forms of energy consumed, food choices, whether your possessions own you, and whether you support leaders who support the planet and the humans who live upon it.

Do your food choices support your own body while causing the least damage to others and the planet? What are you driving, and how frequently? Do you drive ready to compensate for another's mistake or like the road is your personal racetrack? Someday a bicyclist or child may be around that next blind corner. Does your attention and speed allow you to be compassionate toward that unexpected friend? Speaking of bicyclists, how many feet do you give when passing?

How is your phone etiquette? Are you aware that listening to a one-sided conversation is more distracting than listening to two people talking next to you, and that others may not want to hear your conversations? If you are smoking, do you consider who might have to breathe or smell your smoke, even if smoking is allowed?

Do you buy dogs from a breeder or go to the shelter? The issues to ponder are almost limitless. Engage creativity in the quest for light feet. Just as we have enough dogs, we also appear to have enough humans. The walking lightly philosophy can help us contemplate huge choices such as how many copies of us to make. Deciding how many children to have is obviously personal and explosively controversial, but scholars are addressing this issue.[33] Population growth appears to play a role in unsustainable consumption, pollution, and climate change. Thus, it is a legitimate scholarly and ethical question to address exactly how many copies of *me* we need.

Both our genes and culture have evolved to encourage us to believe that parenting is the most responsible and selfless act. Parenting certainly is difficult and selfless, but biological and cultural evolution also program us to believe that parenting our children is the noblest thing we can do. It may be, but we can recognize that parenting is perhaps the most popular meme, meaning it is celebrated and rewarded for strong biological reasons, just as tribal loyalty is. Parenting would be even more compassionate if we decided to adopt as the first option, choosing to nurture an existing child rather than first replicating our genes. However, for the vast majority of people, adopting is not the first choice. Adopting is clearly beautiful. And most people opt to make a child who carries their genes before they consider adopting. The human who is typing is not noble enough to bypass the prime directive, making a copy of me, in favor of adoption as a first-line strategy, yet we

---

[33] The ethics of deciding to have children are discussed in books such as *Why Have Children?: The Ethical Debate* by Christine Overall.

can all rest easy knowing there will not be enough copies of me to form a basketball squad. If you can ponder controversial and brutally difficult questions such as *how many copies of me do we need?* with a lens of walking lightly, then you can certainly decide whether to eat with low impact, drive safely, turn your phone down, or reduce your energy consumption. If we all walk a little lighter, then the earth beneath us, and all those who walk upon it will benefit.

24

Loving-Kindness Meditation

My religion is kindness.

— Tenzin Gyatso, 14th Dalai Lama

Loving-kindness meditation (LKM) has been practiced for thousands of years to transform negative mind states of resentment, anger, and hatred into appreciation, compassion, and love. LKM was developed and refined by Buddhist practitioners, and has now been delivered in western healthcare settings to improve a variety of physical and psychological issues. One does not have to be a Buddhist to practice LKM, as no one has a patent on compassion.[34]

LKM involves generating feelings of kindness, acceptance, and compassion for our selves and then gradually extending these feelings outward in a widening span or circle of compassion. In a typical LKM we first attempt to reconnect with ourselves by recognizing our need for love and compassion. This is not so easy. Many people have a difficult time sending compassion to their self. We need to realize that only when the self is loved and cared for can we move beyond the self to love the world.

---

[34] All the classic spiritual traditions have their own methods for pursuing compassion. Thus, whatever your orientation, LKM will likely be beneficial, and the only known side effects are positive.

After sending compassion to our self, we send compassion toward a series of others further away from the self, such as to one's friends, one's community, all the world's people, all creatures, and finally the entire universe. We build compassion for others at each level by realizing that all people also want love, kindness, and compassion. Just as we do, they wish to be free from suffering and to experience contentment.

By projecting love and kindness outward, we are also being kind to our selves. Sending compassion and kindness outward gives us a break from ego worry and may lessen feelings of separation and isolation, while increasing feelings of happiness and contentment. Reducing resentment and hostility while increasing feelings of compassion and love can transform one's mind and self with obvious benefits to our health.

Loving-Kindness Meditation

Perhaps the best way to experience and learn LKM would be to do it while listening to a teacher, either live, or via an audio recording. You can find many audio tracks by people such as Jon Kabat-Zinn or Sharon Salzberg. I have an LKM audio track at beyondme.life or drweibel.com. On the other hand no audio track is required to begin. LKM and compassion practice are as flexible as the practitioner. You can begin as soon as you set this book down. Below are highlights from one of my scripts, and you can use your imagination to fill in the rest and create your practice.

The first step is to relax and practice mindfulness for a few minutes, coming back to the moment, and honoring the present. Then we imagine a person who loved us well. If we cannot find an example, we can imagine how it would be to be loved well.

LKM script excerpt:

"Consider a person who has loved you well. Recall their acceptance and support. Picture them here, perhaps looking down on you. Soak in these feelings, recalling what it was like to be loved fully. Recall how this person supported you in good times and bad. Recall what love with no or at least few conditions feels like. Bask in what it is like to be accepted despite, and perhaps because of your flaws. Your flaws make you unique, interesting, and lovable.

Now we will shift toward sending compassion to ourselves. Sometimes people have difficulty sending themselves kindness, as they may have been taught that caring for one's self is selfish and that they should spend all their energy caring for others. Within this practice, we realize that in being kind to ourselves, we prepare ourselves to be kind to others, and vice versa. If you are not accustomed to sending kind feelings to yourself, try to make a sincere effort during the exercise.

Realize that you can give unconditional acceptance to yourself, just as the person who loved you did. You can be compassionate toward yourself despite, and perhaps because of your flaws. What you may have previously labeled mistakes may have been a necessary part of your journey that helped make you who you are today. As you send compassion to yourself, you may find it useful to silently say the following intentions or simply hear them and let them resonate.

May I be free from suffering.
May I know peace.
May I experience contentment.

Just let the phrases wash over you. If they feel appropriate then let these intentions and feelings spread within you.

Once again, letting the intentions resonate within.

May I be free from suffering.
May I know peace.
May I experience contentment.

For this chapter, we skip loved ones in the script and jump to community.

Let us extend feelings of loving-kindness to our community. Wishing wellness for the people with whom we interact everyday, often without thinking about them. Your neighbors, your classmates, people with whom you have shared a glance but perhaps never met. The person who serves your morning coffee or delivers your mail, people you work with but have not spoken too, the city workers who clean the streets or janitors who clean your building, endless people who you are connected to and who facilitate your life.

Much of the time, these people do not even enter our consciousness. If we think about them for a moment, however, we realize that just like us, they wish to be free from suffering, to exist in peace, and to find contentment.

Sending them the same acceptance, kindness, and compassion that we sent ourselves.

May my community be free from suffering.
May my community know peace.
May my community experience contentment.

Once again, letting the intentions resonate within.

May my community be free from suffering.
May my community know peace.
May my community experience contentment.

And now we will expand our compassion greatly, moving outward from community to include all communities, all the world's people. Despite tremendous diversity among people and conflicts that arise, we can contemplate that all people share core desires to be free from suffering, to exist in peace, and to find contentment. We can consider that wars are often caused by the

ignorance of large bureaucratic institutions more than evil
in any one person, or that many countries are now allies
with countries that were formerly sworn enemies.
Consider all the people who live in conditions much
harsher than our own, people who are starving or
surrounded by political turmoil and warfare. Attempt to
send acceptance, kindness, and compassion to all the
world's people.

May all people be free from suffering.
May all people know peace.
May all people experience contentment.

Once again, letting the intentions resonate within.

May all people be free from suffering.
May all people know peace.
May all people experience contentment."

Besides expanding the circle of compassion outward
to more people, LKM can also be used to help us lessen
anger and resentment for specific recipients, including
people your mind wants to label an enemy. It is true that
some people are extremely difficult. We will use the
phrase "Person with whom my mind has difficulties"
rather than "My enemy", because doing so acknowledges
the potential role of our perception, biases, and
responsibility. We do not deny that there are evil people
or wrongdoings, yet, it is also true that I let my mind get
angry. Who else would?

Regarding people with whom my mind has difficulties,
we can hold both approximations of truth:

1) There are difficult people, perhaps even evil people, who likely are unlucky in the genetic lottery and were not skillfully loved.

and

2) I am the one responsible for letting my mind get angry. I have the difficulties. I own the difficulties.

Below is an excerpt from a script for how we might extend LKM to a person with whom we have difficulties, or a person whom we have difficulty loving. We should start with a reasonable goal, with someone who we find mildly annoying, not our nemesis, and build our capacity for compassion gradually.

LKM script excerpt:

"Now we will begin the difficult process of attempting to generate forgiveness and acceptance for someone with whom we have difficulties. Picture the person in your mind. Mindfully observe any reactions you have. Does your body grow tense? Does your mind wish to label and condemn the person, creating a convincing case of their flaws like a trial attorney? Just observe your reaction as you picture the person.

Now let's begin pondering how that person came to annoy us. Did our mind play any part in letting ourselves get so annoyed? It may be true that the person did something which others may have called inappropriate, but did our mind rush to label and judge their action, and magnify the offense? The mind likes to be self-protective. In the case of people who annoy us, the mind creates elaborate stories about why they are wrong and we are right. Is there any element of this in your experience?

It is also true that they may have wronged us, hurt us, or done something terrible. Is it possible that they did it because they were hurting? We already recognized that most people want to be free from suffering and to be happy. Is it possible that they were having a hard time meeting those goals and were lashing out in frustration? See if you can step into that person's shoes for a moment and picture their struggle.

Now we will practice a technique called radical acceptance. Radical acceptance involves pondering the fact that we are a result of our genetics and our experience. In many ways we do not have that much control over these. We will ponder that if we had that person's genetics and their upbringing, we would be them. Sit with this. You may even be thankful that you are not that person. But in doing so, can you at least be more forgiving? Can you realize that aspects of their struggle are different than yours? We do not have to condone the person's behavior, but we can make a decision that we will not let our mind be dominated by negative emotions surrounding this person. And now let us recite intentions for the person with whom we have had difficulties:

May the person be free from suffering
May the person know peace
May the person experience contentment.

Letting the intentions resonate as much as possible."

Informal LKM

Just like mindfulness, LKM can be practiced both formally and informally. Formal LKM means a dedicated period of time, in which we sit or lie down and practice. Informal or "off the cushion" practice is the rest of our lives. Thus, we can remember to generate compassion at any moment, and potentially in all moments.

LKM can slice through social awkwardness, mistrust, and animosity. Whenever you are in a bad mood and thinking the world is unfair, and full of ignorant or mean people, practice LKM. Recall past episodes when your mind was in an us versus them mode, such as when you were a newcomer, walked in a room and thought that you were an outsider and that everyone was against you. Once you broke the ice, you realized there was no force field that separated you from them; it was a mental barrier. This fearful social lens could be called 'first day at a new school' mind. If you do not recall what this fearful and awkward mind feels like, go to a nice restaurant or a bar on Saturday night by yourself. You will likely feel or imagine eyes upon you. Practice LKM and those eyes will soften.

In such situations, it is easy to think that the others, the strangers, are evaluating and judging you. This is not the best mindset from which to make friends. Use LKM to increase your trust in the group, the friends you have not yet met. As soon as you feel mentally connected to the group, even if you have not yet spoken to a group member, it becomes easier to make a friend, break in, and enter the group. Feeling connected helps you be connected. Try it, more than once, with an open mind.

25

Serve It Up

Many persons have a wrong idea
of what constitutes true happiness.
It is not attained through self-gratification
but through fidelity to a worthy purpose.

-Hellen Keller

Altruism is the concern for the well being of others
that leads to intentional behaviors that serve or help
others. For our purposes, helping, giving, and serving
overlap with altruism enough to be considered
synonymous. The wisdom of the ages has long encouraged
people to serve others. Aristotle called service,
"Enlightened selfishness." Zoroaster said, "Doing good
deeds for others is not a duty, it is a joy, for it increases
your own health and happiness." Ben Franklin said,
"When you are good to others, you are best to yourself."
Jesus exemplified the golden rule when he recommended,
"Do unto others as you would have them do unto you."

Modern science also indicates that service is not
merely a required extracurricular activity to help
privileged youth get into elite colleges, but is actually a
reliable contributor to life satisfaction, dwarfing the
miniscule satisfaction gains provided by increasing one's
bank account or possessions above subsistence levels.
There is a convincing body of research that helping
others is linked with life satisfaction, contentment,
physical health, and recovery from disease.

Serving gives us a mission and a purpose, something
noble to work for that is larger than our isolated little

self. Serving also ameliorates suffering. People who are suffering often feel helpless and hopeless, and that the world is not meeting their needs. Serving can begin to reverse these beliefs and feelings. It is difficult to feel helpless while helping. Helping almost always benefits the world, even if on a small scale, increasing a sense of hope and optimism in the future and the world. While engaging in meeting the needs of others, it is difficult to remember or notice that the world is not meeting one's needs. In fact, while serving, it is very easy to forget one's self entirely.

Serve it Up

Most of us know how to help, we just see obstacles. By generating some ideas on helping, we might see beyond or around the obstacles.

1. Help via your vocation or avocation

If your job directly involves service, you have a platform. Invest fully in your job, with presence and a deeper intention of helping. Embrace and enhance the service component of your job. Let us not believe that only physicians and baristas are helpful. The person who takes away our garbage is vital. Some of the most honorable people are longtime laborers at jobs that we sometimes overlook. Think of the butterfly effect regarding shoe-shines. A woman gets a shoe-shine, aces the interview, and begins a career from which she supports a family and serves society for forty years. The shine is the butterfly wings flapping.

My uncle Dalmen once wanted to get into a Buddhist monastery, the type of monastery where you have to prove your desire by sitting outside the front gate for days. After that waiting period the monks were deciding if they should let Dalmen in and asked him what he could do to help. In his Navy service, one of his primary jobs was to sweep the deck. Dalmen explained that there is an art to sweeping, and explained that most people just "throw dirt around." He had a method honed by years of Navy sweeping in which he made sweeping interesting by mastering it. He offered to sweep the monastery. The monks were intrigued. Uncle Dalmen got his monastery stay, and the monks learned some subtle sweeping techniques. He embraced a mundane task, served the monastery, and got something back. Do what you do, fully. There is most likely a service component within it.

When you are not working, honor those who are. Appreciate the service you receive every day, from the people who grew and harvested the food you eat to the workers who made the structures that give you shelter. Somebody invented it; somebody made it. Thank them.

2. Volunteer

Volunteering takes many forms. Some people volunteer as a fashion statement and because they have means. Many of the mega-rich do quite a bit of good, and we celebrate the good they accomplish. We also suspect that some of them use their philanthropy as they use art and yachts, as ego-enhancement. Service can also be a means to a partially selfish end. Almost every child who gets into an elite college has arranged to get volunteer experience, as it is as necessary for admittance as their college admission coach. For people with lesser means, it is often difficult to volunteer. To find two extra hours per week is a major struggle. Yet almost everyone would benefit from volunteering.

Many cities now have organizations whose sole function is to connect people wanting to volunteer with organizations wanting volunteers. Go to your local public library and they can connect you with organizations such as Community Literacy Centers, in which you will help a child or adult learn to read.

A great way to volunteer or serve is to teach what you love. Coaching a sport and teaching music are some great avenues. I coached soccer for ten-year-olds for several seasons and can honestly say that coaching soccer

for ten-year-olds was close to the most meaningful and
enjoyable project I have undertaken besides getting
married and having a child. In many ways coaching soccer
was almost as meaningful as earning a Ph.D. Seriously,
the Ph.D. is only ten points above coaching on a
meaningfulness scale. This does not diminish the
doctorate. I loved those children, our team. Your service
will end up high on your ladder, and you will likely make
friends.

3. R.A.K. it up

You can also simply bring more joy to the world via
Random Acts of Kindness (RAK's). RAK's are personal
and situation-based, which is what makes them so fun to
do and to report. The word random in RAK encourages
us to be spontaneous and let it happen. In actuality,
RAK's need not always be random or purely spontaneous.
We can add a systematized part, such as committing to
make every interaction with a stranger today as positive
as possible. What follows is probably the best RAK of the
author's life.

I was on a weekend excursion from my volunteer job
tutoring children in their usual school subjects in Spanish
in the town of Quetzaltenango (Xelajú), Guatemala. After
a night of a wood fired hot-tub and local rum at a
guesthouse, I arose at dawn and paddled my rented kayak
onto Lago de Atitlán, which was guarded by three
volcanoes and had not yet been cursed by jet skis, and
soon came upon two fishermen in their wooden canoes.
The older one proudly showed me his catch of small fish.
He was amazed by the digital pictures I took and showed

them and asked for copies. When asked for his address, he said, "I am Sebastian the fisherman. I live next to the church." After five more amusing minutes of seeking postal clarification, I was satisfied that I had the best address possible and paddled away.

Just as I was about to paddle out of earshot, he said, "Pardon me friend, do you know how I can get a 'thing that ties around your neck?'" He was searching for a "salvavidas" or life jacket for his son who did not know how to swim. His attempts to teach his son to swim had been to no avail, and he had no idea how to get a salvavidas. I was dismayed at the vision of a fisherperson on this massive, often choppy lake who did not know how to swim.

Back at the guesthouse, happily fatigued after four hours of paddling, I planned a nap as the torrential downpour began. The rain stopped after only thirty minutes, and the sunshine overcame my desire to nap. I began to plan a hike. Browsing my map, I realized that Sebastian lived only one town beyond where I had planned to hike, presenting me with a unique opportunity. I had ninety minutes to get a life jacket, run a two-hour hike, find Sebastian, and then catch the last boat back. Luckily, it took me only five minutes to convince one of the hotel workers to sell me a salvavidas.

I began running down the trail with the salvavidas bouncing wildly on top of my pack. After forty minutes the trail became a road, and seven men standing in the back of a truck welcomed me aboard. When the truck stopped, I asked, "Do you know Sebastian 'el pescador'?" "Claro" (Of course). They led me to a house where two older women chuckled at me and instructed two children to lead me to his house. I will never forget the look on Sebastian's face. The whole family was soon outside, and the son put the salvavidas on backwards, with the pontoons pointing behind him. Sebastian kept saying "Te agradezco" (I am grateful). I snapped a photo, made the son promise to learn to swim, and ran for the last boat.

This was my best travel day and one of the best days of my life. I took a chance and connected. It was a win-win. I got joy and a story. Sebastian and his family got a life jacket and a funny memory of the gringo loco.

4.   Be More than Tit for Tat

The leading altruism theorists believe altruism evolved from reciprocity, often summarized by the expression tit for tat. The expectation and practice of getting something in return drove the biological and cultural evolution of altruism. This does not mean that every time we help, we get help in return, but that we realize that having a helping reputation within the tribe is far more valuable than having a non-helping reputation. Like everything, reciprocity is on a continuum.

I once had a friend who told me that for years he had been giving anonymously to various charities at the end of the year. There was no tit for tat with these organizations, as his gift was anonymous. But looking back on it, I was impressed by the story, and when describing this friend to new friends, I described him as honorable, and usually mentioned the anonymous giving, spreading the man's reputation as altruistic. Thus, my friend who mentioned his anonymous giving was getting a bit of tat in the game of tit for tat.

Please experiment with transcending the entire game of tit for tat. Serve with less expectation that your service will be returned. This may mean pulling over and asking strangers with car trouble if they need help, and then providing it. If you live in a decent-sized town, there is little chance that these people will be in your social circle and will increase your reputation. If you did this roadside favor, you might normally tell your friends of your altruistic adventure, but resist the urge.

Other more purely non-reciprocal giving includes such options as leaving a larger tip in a jar when the staff are not looking at who gave it, giving to charity anonymously, picking up garbage on hiking trails, letting drivers merge, and other gestures that you will invent.

Imagine that you were invisible. No one would ever see your helping actions. Nor would your actions be attributable to you. Nothing you ever do would influence your reputation, for you have none, nor would helping enhance your social success or that of your progeny. If reputation is out of the question, do you help as much? People might feel resistance to this thought experiment, but possibly a bit of relief. Many people help because of pressure and reputation. "Be a good girl." Ponder if you would help if you were invisible. It could be fun.

In conclusion, give however much you can. By giving you will usually receive tat for your tit, and will boost your own happiness and likely that of the other. Understand that altruism is both/and, win/win, and non-zero, meaning both giver and receiver benefit. Then push it further; experiment with pure altruism, tit with no tat. See how that feels. Either way, we all benefit.

Expanding
Me

26

One World

*Our task must be to free ourselves by widening our circle of
compassion to embrace all living creatures
and the whole of nature and its beauty.*

- Albert Einstein

If you read this book in a linear fashion, you have
now done some or all of the Compassion Practices.
Hopefully, the human that goes by your name received
some benefit, such as enhancing your empathy, having
less worries, and enjoying more of the small things that
make life worth living.

While many people may have bought this book hoping
to boost happiness or reach self-actualization, it is
important to notice that there is a larger purpose to
compassion practice. While happiness and increased
performance may be side effects of this book, the
intended effect is self-transcendence, which is a step
above or wider than self-actualization. The exercises in
this book were designed to promote perspective taking,
compassion, and expansion from egocentric toward
worldcentric levels of consciousness. When expanding the
self beyond our own concerns, we literally develop our
minds and our consciousness. This is the work and the
journey of the spiritual path. Higher consciousness is
about moving beyond ego to feel less separation, to feel
connected to everything

There are models that describe the path of expanding
compassion, which is synonymous with expanding
consciousness. These models were developed primarily by

the mystics or contemplatives of the classic spiritual traditions. These contemplative scientists, who practiced more than they preached, engaged in rigorous meditative training and then compared notes about the states of consciousness they realized. Contemplatives across different traditions reached a high level of agreement on what constitutes compassion, higher consciousness, or enlightenment.[35] Psychologists and scholars have also codified developmental models that largely overlap with the models developed by contemplatives.

As humans mature and expand their consciousness, they move along a continuum from egocentric, to ethnocentric, to worldcentric levels of consciousness. Ego to Ethno to World. From Me to My tribe to Everybody with subtleties and gradations in between. On the following pages we see two visual representations of the levels along a continuum of consciousness.

---

[35] The field of transpersonal psychology is a great starting point. See Maslow, Ken Wilber, and Graves citations in the Notes.

Expanding Consciousness

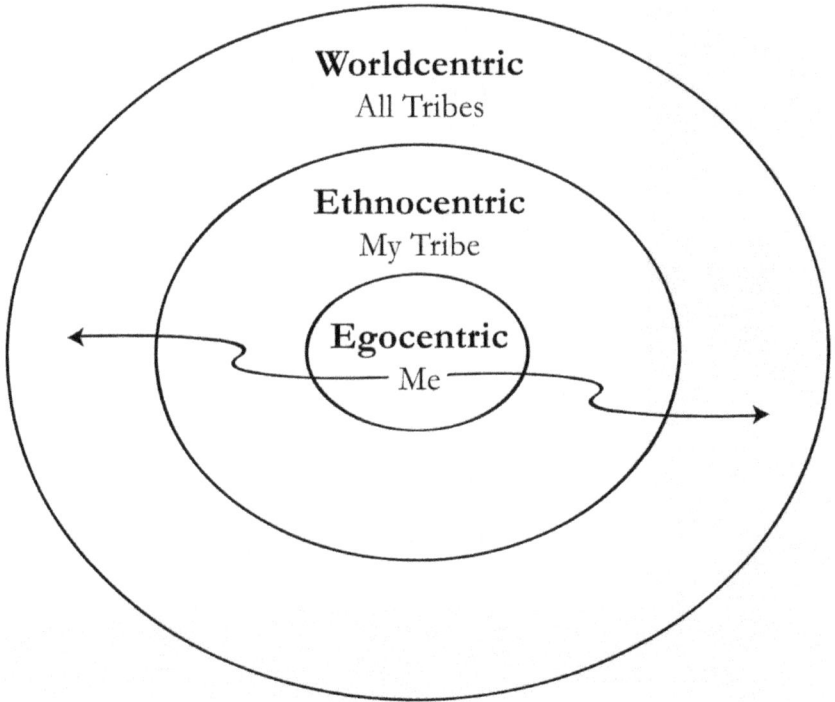

Elevating Consciousness

Levels	Focus	Thought Examples
Enlightenment ~ Cosmocentric	All levels of all people	Love for all levels of development. Zero condemnation of the cocoon that is not yet a butterfly. All levels are necessary steps that every human will go through if we are to reach global consciousness.
	The Universe	Feeling of connectedness to all of life, no boundary, ego has been transcended yet included
Worldcentric	All People	People are more similar than different. All spiritual traditions point toward the same unity.
	Our Planet	We need to teach the ethnocentric people a lesson.
Ethnocentric	My family	They are evil.
	My Tribe	Might makes right.
Egocentric	My needs	Give me candy.
	Me	What did Santa bring me?

We can envision consciousness as elevating upward or expanding outward. The models and the language are equivalent and represent the same process. Choose your metaphor, up or out. Up emphasizes reaching higher levels of consciousness, while out emphasizes a wider embrace, reaching out to encompass the whole planet in one's circle of compassion. Also note that it is basically impossible to skip a level or stage, so you cannot love the planet without first having loved your self and your tribe.

Each person can move between levels of consciousness based on situational variables, but they will have a center of consciousness across the average situation. For example, you can be dedicated to service in your professional and personal life and care deeply for global justice and environmental protection, and still act like a lizard if a thug grabs your girlfriend.

Each person starts out as egocentric. Although children are cute and innocent, ponder for a moment how the average child thinks about their needs and desires come Christmas time. The child is out for me and mine. Extremely rare is the child who says, "I don't want any presents this year. I would like to give the money that would have been spent on my presents to a charity feeding starving children." A child who says this likely heard about such an act and has deduced that the parents are going to greatly reward this generous demonstration. Children are cute, innocent, and lovable. And manipulative and selfish. I want candy. Give me candy. Now.

After egocentric comes the ethnocentric stage, in which we identify with our family, country, school, team or other tribal association. We become part of something greater than our selves, and show extreme loyalty and love to this larger entity. We can even treat the tribe and ideas associated with it as sacred. People feel deeply proud when their country wins a major international sporting event. Feeling national pride is a positive and pleasurable step. While this level is not as broad as global consciousness, it is necessary to move toward global consciousness. You have to love one tribe before you love all tribes. You have to love a team before you love all teams, all games, and all players.

After ethnocentric comes worldcentric, or global consciousness. At this level I can still love my home country or team, but I also love all countries. Because consciousness always expands in a manner that transcends and includes, you can be at worldcentric and love everybody, and still relish the joy of your home team winning. You still include the younger you, the tribal you, who grew up loving one team. However, the wider you loves the game itself and everybody who has ever played or could play.

At worldcentric, I include the nationalistic me who loves my country, but I do not think my country was somehow blessed to have more innate qualities, rights, and privileges than other countries. At this level I can appreciate and cherish the diversity of people. I clearly see that some people have been oppressed more than others. These currently oppressed or previously oppressed people may rightly not want to be immediately lumped into a global civilization or universal consciousness, as they sill want their own struggle to be recognized and rectified. We understand and respect their wishes. And, from a worldcentric perspective we can also realize that at basic levels, such as wanting to be loved, we are all the same, or at least highly similar.

Consciousness at this level is similar to the pictures from outer space that look down on the earth. From this height, the Earth is clearly one planet with no borders or nations. All the oceans are one body of water. The air is also one atmosphere. At this level we have planetary consciousness. We realize the 'sisterhood of man.' We are one species, one tribe, riding this rock through space.

Beyond worldcentric lies cosmocentric, the first stage in which people could be called enlightened. These people have worldcentric values but have added one important distinction, a wider, fuller, and deeper understanding of the entire spiral or spectrum of development. Everyone, who is pre-enlightenment, including a person with worldcentric consciousness tends to judge the other levels. This is why a person with worldcentric consciousness will often condemn and judge the people with ethnocentric or egocentric consciousness. A person with worldcentric consciousness is as intolerant of racists, sexists, and homophobes as racists, sexists, and homophobes are of the targets of their discrimination.

The enlightened individual loves the entire spiral or spectrum of development and thus does not violently condemn people at egocentric or ethnocentric levels, even someone displaying offensive beliefs, including racist beliefs. This does not mean that the enlightened person cannot discern differences, have preferences, or take action to stop abhorrent behaviors. But they do not take the behaviors personally, nor do they act punitively with the intent to destroy a person. The enlightened person understands that saying they hate egocentric people is like saying they hate six-year-olds or first graders. Obviously, they do not hate all six-year-olds or first graders. Enlightened people, and really most people, love six-year-

olds. We all were in first grade once, and every new
member of the human race will go through first grade or
its equivalent. First grade, just like egocentric and
ethnocentric consciousness, are vital steps in each
individual's progression and evolution of consciousness.
Without first grade, or the egocentric level of
consciousness, there are no higher stages. There are no
skyscrapers without ground floors.

Enlightenment could be exemplified by how the Dalai
Lama does not appear to hate the Chinese government for
invading and re-populating Tibet while destroying
thousands of temples. He disapproves of the action and
takes steps to remedy it, but does not appear to have a
deep hatred for the Chinese leaders who made the
decision to invade his country and appeared to be acting
from egocentric and ethnocentric consciousness. At no
point does higher consciousness prevent us from taking
action. In fact, higher consciousness leads to wise action.

The compassionate path involves moving from ego to
ethno to world to cosmo by expanding our perspective,
empathy, and compassion. The spiritual path that the
consciousness models represent provides us hope because
we see that that there is a path walked by thousands of
contemplatives and practitioners in the present day and
across history. These paths or maps also give us a sense
of community, as we know that millions of previous
seekers have raised their consciousness. At any one time
or place, the path can seem lightly trodden, and it can be
lonely to be a spiritual seeker within a society with
materialistic and narcissistic leanings, where celebrity
magpies are famous for being famous, and farcical
mutations of religions promise that God wants you to be
rich or lead to violence against out-groups. Despite the

potential loneliness in compassion practice, all evidence indicates that more and more people are interested in raising their consciousness. If you choose the path that can appear less traveled by, you will be in good company and will be less alone with passing time as more and more people are practicing compassion.

At first, moving beyond me seems like a burden. You might ask, "I can barely take care of my self, how can I care for the entire world?" Relax and realize you will not have to solve the entire world's problems, at least not in one fell gesture, and at least not by your lonesome.

If you raise your consciousness, you will be able to consider and empathize with the entire world. You will no longer divide people into us versus them so easily. Your categories will have expanded in addition to your consciousness. Your us will be a far wider category, including more people and things. Your me will be less narrow, insecure, and loud.

Once you embrace the wider view and expand your compassion, you will feel more pain, but you will suffer less. This is a good thing. You will feel more pain because you are concerned with the entire world's suffering. You pay more attention and notice when tragedies both near and far occur. You will suffer less, as your compassion will be wider and you will be able to transform suffering into positive intentions and emotions. You will project compassion toward others' suffering and will take action where you can, but you will not absorb or identify with the suffering to the point of overwhelming your empathic capacity. Thus, you can witness and attend to pain, but you will not suffer as much. You can even feel meaning and contentment as you generate compassion for others.

You will suffer less because suffering is the dis-ease of the ego. Worry, anxiety, neurosis and depression are ego-based. Suffering arises when you make judgments and evaluations of your self. Suffering comes from being tied up in your own miserable ego story, in which you are a separate and isolated self in a hostile world.

Once you have developed wide compassion, you will be more steady, as you will be less upset by the vicissitudes of your little ego story. Assume you make a faux pas at a party. When you are as concerned about the most recent genocide as you are about how your party banter was received, then your evaluation of your self-perceived faux pas will be less likely to affect you. Both the genocide and your faux pas now fall within the wider scope of your flexible identity and wider compassion. You will not self-flagellate for whatever you said, and you will likely not even label it a faux pas, as you now have a deeper compassion for everyone including yourself and your ego story. When trapped in your ego, you are a boat on a turbulent ocean. When you move beyond me, reaching wider consciousness and compassion, you are the ocean. Your surface may get choppy, but your depths are calm.

When we are absorbed in our ego struggles, we are less present to connect with others. When I get outside my struggle, I can consider others and bond with them. This can gain momentum in a cyclical manner, as social support lessen self-focused angst. Connectedness lessens self-absorption, enabling present-focus and receptivity, which enables connectedess. In the words of one of my former students "Having a faith on somebody, believing on them safes us from having wrinkle on our face."[36]

---

[36] Rabin was a Nepalese exchange student when this writer asked students to complete five of the practices in this book. His awesome effort in the experiential exercises overcame any grammar errors.

27

The Direction is Up

Global consciousness for global problems

The overall, long-term, average direction for humanity is up or wider in terms of consciousness, empathy, and compassion. The average person today is more compassionate than an average person who lived 50, 200, 1,000, or 10,000 years ago. There are also more people living and thinking at higher levels of consciousness than 1,000 years ago. These high consciousness humans, experts in empathic reasoning, are still less than 10% of the population, but 3,000 years ago, they were likely less than 1% of the population. So there are thousands of enlightened people among us and millions who are on the path, aiming to live with global consciousness.

More good news is that a small but influential and enthusiastic minority is all that is typically needed to shift society in a direction that soon becomes the majority or norm. Around two hundred years ago, small but influential minorities emerged who realized the necessity of ending legal slavery and of promoting women's equality. Once the progress-focused activists gained momentum, it was almost inevitable that these beliefs and practices will become the beliefs held by the majority and eventually the norm. Marketers have long known this. Once you get the right 15% of people to adopt a new trend, the momentum and inertia have begun, and soon the later adopters will also be embracing the new technology or meme. The theory is the same with social change.

One way to enhance and leverage change is to recognize where it has already been made. Today, if you were to say, "I want to buy a slave to help out my old lady" today among anyone with an average level of consciousness, you will be ridiculed and avoided. So rather than think that the people at a worldcentric level of consciousness are outnumbered, which they are, realize the average consciousness is rising and may be within range of reaching a tipping point in which a truly global or empathic civilization can be realized.

The world is also more peaceful now than it was 200, 2,000, or 10,000 years ago. With the lens of millennia, we see humans and societies evolve. Individuals or even nations and regions can stagnate or even backslide, but the long-term direction has been up. Despite the evidence that the world is getting better, many people believe the world is going to hell in a handbasket, and that humans are getting worse.

There are several reasons why it is hard to believe the world is getting better. First, people have a tendency to long for their own good ol' days, the days of their youth, and tend to always think it was better then, just as they often think the young people now are lazy. Another reason is that some scholars also have intentionally or unintentionally glorified earlier societies and present day societies still living in hunter-gatherer ways, as living peacefully in harmony with nature, sometimes to be corrupted by an outside modern force. Some of these well-meaning anthropologists and ethnographers appeared to have become so deeply involved with their subjects, that they filtered data with their own biases and portrayed

these societies as incredibly peaceful, only later to have
their data corrected by later researchers, who revealed
that hunter gatherer tribes can be every bit as bloody as
the modern people, if not more so.[37]

Another factor making it difficult to believe that
progress happens, is that the progress is almost always
drowned out by bad news, whose producers know that
death and catastrophe are more unique and out of the
ordinary than a billion daily kindnesses, and thus more
likely to attract eyeballs. To understand why negative
events are more newsworthy, just think about a headline
entitled, "Young lady helps old man across street." The
news companies broadcast the most shocking bad things
that happen across the entire globe each day. The law of
large numbers reveals that when a sample size is large
enough, you will find most possible events within that
sample size. If the sample size is seven billion people and
each person experiences ten events per day, then the
sample size is seventy billion events. Almost anything
possible will happen within that sample, including good
things. At least 100 people found $100 today. 100 people
fell in love today. And 100 people were killed today. This
does not mean the world is getting worse. The global
news is indeed all bad, as many bad things happen every
day with a sample size of all events across the entire
globe.

Despite the fact that one can find bad events that
happen in the world each day, those bad events, best
exemplified by violence, are actually decreasing. Hate is

---

[37] See Freeman, D. (1983). Margaret Mead and Samoa. Freeman returned 20 years
later to replicate and extend Mead's research. He spent more time than her and
learned that her subjects had thought it was a fun game to fabricate stories for the
strange researcher from a distant land.

certainly awful, but violence is hate operationalized. Stephen Pinker's authoritative *The Better Angels of Our Nature: Why Violence Has Declined* integrates data from fields such as anthropology, forensic archaeology, military history, criminology, and atrocitology to make a convincing case that human violence is decreasing. Acts of violence are countable, and they have decreased dramatically. In the field of forensic anthropology, researchers find the cause of death on fossilized humans by finding spear and other weapon marks on the skeletons. Researchers also study the several remaining tribes that appear to still live as humans did thousands of years ago. Combining all the data Pinker found that in the 20th century, including both World Wars, the chance of being killed by another human was far below 1%. In hunter-gatherer tribes that represent our origins, the odds of dying at the end of a spear were 15%.

Our minds are strongly influenced by the most recent violent news image we see to believe that the world is going to the wolves. Yet the evidence clearly shows that we are more peaceful than we have ever been. If you doubt this, read history and then meditate on what it was like to live 500 years ago, or 10,000 years ago, or 100,000 years ago.

Despite the fact that per capita acts of violence have decreased dramatically, ever-increasing technology and more lethal weapons do allow for the possibility that a few psychopaths or fanatics can do massive damage via terror, or biological or nuclear weapons. So now is not quite the time to celebrate. As discussed before, we also now may have much bigger problems than violence, such as degrading the environment so badly that the earth may not be able to sustain human life for another millennia, whether we are peaceful or violent. There are also credible scenarios whereby climate change will lead to scarcity of land, resources, and food, and that this scarcity will lead to subsequent violence.

Still, for those who had been good ol' biased and media-washed to believe the doomsday scenarios, the evidence that the world is getting less violent and that human culture and consciousness evolves is heartening and motivating. A decrease in violence is not the only sign of progress. The rights revolutions, consisting of increases in empathy and rights for minorities, women, children, LGBT folks, and animals have all occurred within a blink of an eye in terms of human history. The chronological order of the rights revolutions was slaves, women, children, people identifying as LGBT, and animals. The reasoning within the rights revolutions was largely transferrable as each revolution provided a model that could be duplicated or extended. These rights revolutions were based on discoveries or innovations not that different from the discovery that gravity exists or the earth is round. Many ancient peoples thought earthquakes were caused by angry gods. It took reasoning, inventions, and discoveries to learn that this was not that case and provide a more accurate causal explanation. As little as three hundred years ago many people had not discovered the basic principle or reasoning behind equal rights. Three hundred years ago, a king, church leader, or similarly privileged and educated person would be considered morally challenged or ignorant by today's standards, in that they might own slaves, deny women the vote, whip children, bully gays, and torture animals. And they would not have to hide their behaviors; you could be at the peak of society three hundred years ago and hold views that are now deemed barbaric. These earlier people also had reasons, poor ones by today's culturally evolved standards, for their morality. In 1837, John Calhoun, a senator from South Carolina rationalized slavery in a speech to the United States Congress, saying "I appeal to facts. Never before has the black race of Central Africa, from the dawn of history to the present day, attained a condition so civilized and so improved, not only physically, but morally and intellectually. It came among us in a low, degraded, and savage condition, and in the course of a few generations it has grown up under the fostering care of our institutions, reviled as they have been, to its present comparatively civilized condition. This, with the rapid increase of numbers, is conclusive proof of the general happiness of the race, in spite of all the exaggerated tales to the contrary."

Sir, the "facts", as you called them, have changed. So has our ability to reason as well as the level of reasoning in the culture, specifically surrounding rights. In the past arguments were made that a woman's natural position was to silently serve. Today, we have more sources, more knowledge, and better reasoning. Today older justifications for keeping slaves or treating your wife like property hold as much cred as saying the world is flat. Human knowledge and reasoning has increased, and it has lead to innovations such as the principle of universal human rights. Progress has occurred.

Today any vociferous rights advocate might resist the idea of celebrating progress and and say 'look how much remains to be done.' Certainly. We still have a long way to go. And we can recognize that the lack of satisfaction at progress to date and outrage at the still existent oppression, are themselves features of progress. Current outrage is like a refined taste in the realm of rights and reasoning about rights. Because progress has been made in the realm of rights, compassionate people are now more finely able to recognize and get outraged about violations they see.

Progress has also been made toward sustainable energy and reducing emissions. Denmark had a day in 2015 in which they produced 140% of their energy needs from wind turbines. Germany has dedicated itself to the Energiewende, a transition to renewable sources of energy and has made significant progress. The United States is lagging a bit, but we if we got as motivated and competitive about sustainable energy as we have about other things such as the Super Bowl or the Space Race, then we would have a better chance, and everyone might benefit. We might even decide to collaborate.

The evidence of progress within history such as the rights revolutions, as well as more recent technological progress, provides hope, and this hope and sense of community should support the people trying to raise their consciousness and build the global civilization. More and more people want to expand their compassion and open to higher consciousness. The more people get to worldcentric consciousness, the more we can cooperate, and pursue non-zero or win-win outcomes. Our subsequent books and essays will address specific personal and social actions that we can take. This book is more about the foundational task of raising our level of consciousness and achieving a non-zero mindset, in which the main goal is to make life livable and pleasant for as many of the world's creatures as possible.

The more people expand to worldcentric, the more obvious the solutions to the world's problems will be, or

at least we will be on the same team looking for solutions.
Reaching higher consciousness is not likely to create a
vibration that magically solves problems far away from
the high consciousness minds, but we can and should
realize that having worldcentric leaders is far more
effective than having tribal-centric leaders fighting wars
to expand collective ego, financial interests, or belief
systems. Looking at history, we can see that a majority of
the violence and destruction was driven by insecure and
compensatorily inflated ego and collective ego. To
someone at a worldcentric level of consciousness,
fighting aggressive battles over possessions, turf, religion,
$, race, nation, sexuality, and other distinctions is about
as reasonable and productive as a fútbol team whose
players decide to start shooting on their own goal. For
the non-fútbolistas, the aforementioned ego squabbles
would be as illogical as a football receiver who decides
not to catch the quarterback's passes because they had a
tiff. The receiver catches passes thrown by their
quarterback and the soccer player shoots on the other
team's goal because it is good for them personally and for
their team collectively. It is the reasonable thing to do.

The same loyalty that you feel to your family or your
favorite team, a worldcentric person feels to everybody.
This is a better position from which to foster the
cooperation needed to solve the world's issues. Let us use
one of the environmental movement's early struggles as
an example for how changes in consciousness facilitate
behavior change and real-world solutions. Forty years ago,
before scientists had sounded the alarm on climate change,
litter was higher on a list of environmental problems. Not
chemical runoff from factories, which was also a huge
problem, but individuals throwing their garbage out the

window on the road, or in the creek rather than using trash cans. The environmental movement originally tried to preach to and scold people, telling them, "Don't pollute." This did not have success. Don'ts rarely do. Shaming people usually increases the behavior you are trying to reduce.

Empathy works much better. The environmental movement had much better luck when they tried to help us empathize with other humans and nature, rather than scolding us. The crying Native American commercial was emblematic of this movement. Regardless of whether this public service announcement was politically correct or of good production value by today's standards, the commercial and related campaigns had more of an effect than previous scolding campaigns. The ad showed a close-up of an actor playing a Native American who was crying because the land had been polluted and ruined. If the Native American's sadness resonates with you, you feel what he feels. You realize his pain is yours, and now you automatically do not litter, because his pain is yours; his Earth is yours. It is ours, and we do not throw trash in our own living rooms. There is less need for prohibition, scolding, or don'ts when we have empathy and ownership. This ad is regarded as a successful public service announcement, as it apparently contributed to behavior change. Littering is far less of a problem than it used to be.

When consciousness changes to include the others' feelings and their interests, protecting the other, who is no longer considered an other, is automatic. Once your consciousness changes, caring for the planet is as obvious as brushing your teeth. You never go days without brushing. Why? Because it is messy. So is polluting the earth, our planet. Just as you feel and care for your body, when your consciousness expands you will feel and care for the earth and its inhabitants.

There are obviously problems on our planet bigger than litter. The solutions will be complex, requiring our best and brightest minds, reason, science, compassion, and effective organizations. Some people might say consciousness expansion is less efficient than political and social action. By no means has the point of this book been against political or social action. The point of this book is to transform one's consciousness and engage. You can also alternate between the two, nurture compassion, deliver compassion, or do both at the same time. For example, practicing altruism helps others while expanding your heart and consciousness.

Higher consciousness is the foundation of wise action. Spirituality is sustenance for the soul and for soulful action, not a dreamy vision of celestial dancers on moonbeams. Compassion practice is not woo-woo crystal-rubbing fairy dust. Wider compassion frees us to solve the actual problems of the world rather than squabbling over conflicting ego stories. We need to be less tribal and more global, conscious, and moral. Having the capacity to hold more perspectives, to resonate with empathy, to deliver compassion, is the central component of emotional intelligence, maturity, morality, and wisdom that we need in effective citizens and leaders of all types. It is the key to personal satisfaction and meaningful lives as well as the basis for a co-existence with our fellow bipeds. When we understand that connectedness is the governing principle of everything, we choose strategies where more people win more of the time. Moving beyond me is perhaps the most important thing one can do to be

a stalwart global family member, to help us thrive. It also
enhances dancing. Boogie on.

Recommended

Mindfulness & Compassion

The Art of Forgiveness, Lovingkindness, & Peace by Jack Kornfield

Wherever You Go, There You Are & *Full Catastrophe Living* by Jon Kabat-Zinn

Tao Te Ching by Lao Tzu, translation by Stephen Mitchell

Lovingkindness: The Revolutionary Art of Happiness by Sharon Salzberg

Thoughts Without a Thinker by Mark Epstein

Peace Is Every Step: The Path of Mindfulness by Thich Nhat Hanh

The Inner Game by Timothy Gallwey

Mindful Discipline: A Loving Approach to Setting Limits by Shauna Shapiro

The Lost Art of Compassion by Lorne Ladner

The Wisdom of Insecurity: A Message for an Age of Anxiety by Alan Watts

Seeds of Contemplation by Thomas Merton

Get Out of Your Mind and Into Your Life by Stephen Hayes

Radical Acceptance by Tara Brach

Field Notes on the Compassionate Life by Marc Barasch

Self-Compassion by Kristin Neff

God is a Verb by David Cooper

The Power of Now by Eckhart Tolle

Zen in the Art of Archery by Eugen Herrigel

Progress

Non-Zero: The Logic of Human Destiny by Robert Wright

Angels of Our Nature: Why Violence Has Declined by Steven Pinker

The Moral Landscape: How Science Can Determine Values by Sam Harris

The Empathic Civilization by Jeremy Rifkin

The Expanding Circle by Peter Singer

Moral Tribes by Joshua Greene

The Moral Arc by Michael Shermer

Center for Compassion & Altruism Research & Education (ccare.standord.edu)

Greater Good, The Science of a Meaningful Life (greatergood.berkeley.edu)

Transpersonal Psychology

The Farther Reaches of Human Nature by Abraham Maslow

The Evolution of God by Robert Wright

Sex, Ecology, & Spirituality: The Evolution of Spirit by Ken Wilber

Waking Up: A Guide to Spirituality without Religion by Sam Harris

The Perennial Philosophy: An Interpretation of the Great Mystics by Aldous Huxley

Spiritual Evolution: How We Are Wired for Faith, Hope, and Love by G. Vaillant

Essential Spirituality: 7 Central Practices to Awaken Heart & Mind by R. Walsh

The Self

Escaping the Self by Robert Baumeister

The Curse of the Self by Mark Leary

The Narcissism Epidemic by Jean Twenge & W. Campbell

The Protean Self by Robert J. Lifton

Meaning

Man's Search for Meaning by Victor Frankl

The Myth of Sisyphus by Albert Camus

Existential Psychotherapy by Irvin Yalom

The Meaning of Anxiety by Rollo May

Ecopsychology

The Voice of the Earth: An Exploration of Ecopsychology by Theodore Roszak

Last Child in the Woods by Richard Louv

Six Degrees: Our Future on a Hotter Planet by Mark Lynas

The Sixth Extinction: An Unnatural History by Elizabeth Kolbert

Forgiveness, Gratitude, Altruism, & Happiness

Five Steps to Forgiveness: The Art & Science of Forgiveness by Worthington

Forgive for Good by Frederic Luskin

Thanks!: How the New Science of Gratitude Can Make You Happier by Emmons

Naikan: Gratitude, Grace, and the Japanese Art of Self-Reflection by Gregg Krech

Why Good Things Happen to Good People by Stephen Post & Jill Neimark

The Geography of Bliss: One Grump's Search for the Happiest Places... by Weiner

Flourish: A Visionary New Understanding of Happiness and Well-being by Seligman

The Happiness Hypothesis By Jonathan Haidt

Bright-Sided: How Positive Thinking Is Undermining America by Ehrenreich

Fun

Wabi Sabi for Artists, Designers, Poets, & Philosophers by Leonard Koren

The Dice Man by Luke Rhinehart

Coyote Blue & *The Lust Lizard of Melancholy Cove* by Christopher Moore

The Tao of Pooh by Benjamin Hoff

The Dilbert Principle by Scott Adams

Skinny Legs and All by Tom Robbins

Letters to a Young Poet by Rainer Maria Rilke

The Little Hummingbird by Michael Yahgulanaas

Notes

2   **Oxford dictionary defines compassion as....**

www.oxforddictionaries.com accessed 6/2015.

5   **Dr. Larry Scherwitz, examining the risk factors...**

Scherwitz, L. & Canick, J. (1988). Self-reference and coronary heart disease risk. *Type A behavior pattern: Research, theory, and intervention,* Kent, H. & Snyder, C. (Eds.), pp. 146-167. Oxford, England: John Wiley & Sons.

7   **Oxford dictionary defines the self as....**

www.oxforddictionaries.com accessed 6/2015.

8   **Ken Wilber coined the phrase...**

Wilber, Ken. (1995). *Sex, Ecology, and Spirituality: The Spirit of Evolution.* Boston, MA: Shambhala Publications.

10   **letting us practice effortless effort...**

Mitchell, S. (1989). *Tao Te Ching: A New English Version.* New York: Harpercollins.

16   **How the Self Helps Us? - chapter synthesizes & builds upon:**

Leary, M. (2007). *The Curse of the Self: Self-Awareness, Egotism, and the Quality of Human Life.* Cary, North Carolina: Oxford University Press.

Baumeister, R. (1991). *Escaping the Self: Alcoholism, Spirituality, Masochism, and Other Flights from the Burden of Selfhood.* New York: Basic Books.

Baumeister, R. & Tierney, J. (2012). *Willpower: Rediscovering the Greatest Human Strength.* New York: Penguin Books.

Vohs, K. & Baumeister, R. (Eds.) (2013) *Handbook of Self-Regulation, Second Edition: Research, Theory, and Applications.* New York: The Guilford Press.

Researchers studying the influence of options on...

Iyengar, S. & Lepper, M. (2000). When choice is demotivating: Can one desire too much of a good thing? *Journal of Personality and Social Psychology,* 79(6), 995-1006.

Schwartz, B. (2005). *The Paradox of Choice: Why More Is Less.* New York: Harper Perennial.

20   **A rapidly growing body of research...**

Waal, F. (2009). *The Age of Empathy: Nature's Lessons for a Kinder Society.* New York: Broadway Books.

Bloom, P. (2013). *Just Babies: The Origins of Good and Evil.* New York: Crown

Publishing.

Rifkin, J. (2009). *The Empathic Civilization: The Race to Global Consciousness in a World in Crisis*. New York, NY: Tarcher.

When toddlers see a person in pain...

Zahn-Waxler, C., Radke-Yarrow, M., Wagner, E., Chapman, M. (1992). Development of Concern for Others. *Developmental Psychology*, 28, 126-36.

In another experiment, if an adult drops a pen...

Warneken, F. & Tomasello, M. (2006) Altruistic Helping in Human Infants and Young Chimpanzees. *Science*, 311, 1301-1303.

In another study babies watch movies in which one...

Kuhlmeier, V., Wynn, K., Bloom, P. (2003) Attribution of dispositional states by 12-month-old infants, *Psychological Science*, 14, 402-408.

21   **Children as young as three months old**

Hamlin, J.K., Wynn, K., & Bloom, P (2010) 3-Month-Olds show a negativity bias in social evaluation. *Developmental Science*, 13, 923-939.

In a similar research design a puppet struggles to lift...

Hamlin, J.K., Wynn, K., & Bloom, P. (2007) Social evaluations by preverbal infants, *Nature*, 450, 557-59.

In an extension of the lid-slamming and ball-stealing

Hamlin, J.K., Wynn, K., & Bloom, P., Mahajan, N. (2011). How infants and toddlers react to antisocial others. *Proceedings of the National Academy of Sciences*, 108, 19931-19936.

22   **Studies have shown that people vary on their levels...**

Baron-Cohen,S. (1997). *Mindblindness: An Essay on Autism and Theory of Mind*. Colorado: Bradford Publishing. Book.

24   **This ability to engage in hypotheticals...**

Zare, A., Shahin, N., Shahla, R. & Iran, K. (2012). Autistic children and different tense forms. *World Academy of Sciences, Engineering, and Technology*. 70, 72-76.

26   **The mind will see danger where there is none...**

Schoen, M. (2013). *Your Survival Instinct Is Killing You: Retrain Your Brain to Conquer Fear, Make Better Decisions, and Thrive in the 21st Century*. New York: Hudson Street Press.

28   **The fear response is much stronger...**

Baumeister, R., Bratslavsky, E., Finkenauer, C., & Vohs, K. (2001). Bad is

Stronger than Good. *Review of General Psychiatry*, 5 (4), 323-370.

30 **I've had many troubles; some actually...**

Powers, R. (2006). *Mark Twain: A Life*. New York: Free Press

Anxiety and depression or mood disorders are...

http://www.hcp.med.harvard.edu/wmh/index.php

32 **Although psychological conditions have genetic and biological**

Satel, S. & Lilienfeld, S. O. (2013). *Brainwashed: The Seductive Appeal of Mindless Neuroscience*. New York: Basic Books.

Kirsch, I. (2010). *The Emperor's New Drugs: Exploding the Antidepressant Myth*. New York: Basic Books.

Whitaker, R. (2011). *Anatomy of an Epidemic: Magic Bullets, Psychiatric Drugs, and the Astonishing Rise of Mental Illness in America*. New York: Broadway Books.

Breggin, P. & Cohen, D. (2007). *Your Drug May Be Your Problem: How and Why to Stop Taking Psychiatric Medications*. Boston: MA: Da Capo Press.

Petersen, M. (2008). *Our Daily Meds: How the Pharmaceutical Companies Transformed Themselves into Slick Marketing Machines and Hooked the Nation on Prescription Drugs*. New York: Farrar, Straus and Giroux.

Gotzsche, P. (2013). *Deadly Medicines and Organised Crime: How Big Pharma Has Corrupted Healthcare*. London, UK: Radcliffe Medical Press Limited.

33 **Today you might get as anxious when a coworker**

Glassner, B. (2010). *The Culture of Fear: Why Americans Are Afraid of the Wrong Things*, revised edition. New York: Basic Books.

Sapolsky, R. (2004). *Why Zebras Don't Get Ulcers*. New York: Holt.

34 **based on and modified from cognitive therapy...**

Beck, J. & Beck, A. (2011). *Cognitive Behavior Therapy: Basics and Beyond* (2nd Edition) New York: The Guilford Press.

39 **A tree that cannot bend will crack in the wind.**

Mitchell, S. (1989). *Tao Te Ching: A New English Version*. New York: Harpercollins.

42 **For what shall it profit a man,...**

The Holy Bible: Containing the Old and New Testaments in the Authorized King James Version. Easton Press. (1990).

Once you have met the basic needs...

Kasser, T. & Kanner, A. (2003). *Psychology and Consumer Culture: The Struggle for a Good Life in a Materialistic World.* Washington, DC: American Psychological Association.

44   Pray that your loneliness may spur you...

Hammarskjöld, D. (1976). *Markings.* New York: Alfred A. Knopf.

people who are high in loneliness have higher...

Cacioppo, J. & William, P. (2009). *Loneliness: Human Nature and the Need for Social Connection,* New York: W. W. Norton & Company.

there has been a dramatic decrease in community

Putnam, R. (2000). *Bowling Alone: The Collapse and Revival of American Community.* New York: Simon & Schuster.

45   "Personal relations founded on reflected glory...

Lasch, C. (1978). *The Culture of Narcissism: American Life in an Age of Diminishing Expectations.* New York: W. W. Norton & Company.

47   when asked what they were thinking during their flow

Williams, J. (2009). *Applied Sports Psychology: Personal Growth to Peak Performance,* 6th edition. New York: McGraw-Hill.

Csikszentmihalyi, M. (1990). *Flow: The Psychology of Optimal Experience.* New York: Harpercollins.

48   Artists report that creative bursts arrive...

Cameron, J. (2002). *The Artist's Way.* 10th edition. New York: Tarcher.

49   A man wrapped up in himself makes a very small bundle.

Isaacson, W. (2004). *Benjamin Franklin: An American Life.* New York: Simon & Schuster.

The Narcissistic Personality Inventory has been given

Twenge, J. & Campbell, W. (2010). *The Narcissism Epidemic: Living in the Age of Entitlement.* New York: Atria Books.

Twenge, J. (2007). *Generation Me: Why Today's Young Americans Are More Confident, Assertive, Entitled-and More Miserable Than Ever Before,* New York: Atria Books.

self-reported empathy has declined since 1980

Konrath, S., O'Brien, E. & Hsing, C. (2011). Changes in dispositional empathy in American college students over time: a meta-analysis. *Personality and Social Psychology Review,* 15 (2), 180-198.

50   The movement to boost self-esteem took hold...

Kohn, A. (1999). *Punished by Rewards: The Trouble with Gold Stars, Incentive*

Plans, A's, Praise, and Other Bribes, 2 edition. New York: Mariner Books.

51   **Below is a song sung to...**

www.childcarelounge.com/general-themse/i-am-special.php on 5/15/15

54   **If you go back in time you will find tribes...**

Singer, P. (2011) *The Expanding Circle: Ethics, Evolution, and Moral Progress.*
Princeton, New Jersey: Princeton University Press.

55   **In a series of experiments Henri Tajfel...**

Tajfel , H. (1981). *Human Groups and Social Categories: Studies in Social
Psychology.* Cambridge, UK: Cambridge University Press

      In the classic Robbers Cave Experiment...

Sherif, M. Harvey, O., White, B, Hood, W. & Sherif, C. (1954/1961).
*Study of positive and negative intergroup attitudes between experimentally produced
groups: Robbers Cave study.* Norman, Oklahoma: University of Oklahoma.

61   **An experiment with mice reveals...**

Couppis, M. & Kennedy, C. (2008). The rewarding effect of aggression is
reduced by nucleus accumbens dopamine receptor antagonism in mice.
Psychopharmacology, 197(3), 449-456.

62   **Women traditionally fought less with fists...**

Greiling, H. & Buss, D. (2000) Women's sexual strategies: The hidden
dimension of extra-pair mating. *Personality and Individual Differences*, 28(5),
929-963.

Ridley, M. (1994). *The Red Queen: Sex and the Evolution of Human Nature.* New
York: Macmillan Publishing Company.

64   **The optimistic news is that the per capita...**

Pinker, S. (2012). *The Better Angels of Our Nature: Why Violence Has Declined.*
New York: Penguin Books.

65   **We abuse land because we see it as a commodity...**

Leopold, A. (2001). *A Sand County Almanac: With Essays on Conservation.*
Cary, North Carolina: Oxford University Press.

      The biosphere may have already crossed...

Barnoksy, A., Hadly, E., Bascompte, J., Berlow, E., Brown, J., Fortelius, M.,
Getz, W., Harte, J., Hastings, A., Marquet, P., Martinez, N., Mooers, A.,
Roopnarine, P., Vermeij, G., Williams, J., Gillespie, R., Kitzes, J., Marshall,
C., Matzke, N., Mindell, D., Revilla, E. & Smith, A. (2012). Approaching a
state shift in Earth's biosphere. *Nature*, 486 (7401), 52-58.

have funding ties to political interest groups...

Dunlap, R. & McCright, A. (2011). Organized Climate Change Denial. *The Oxford Handbook of Climate Change and Society*. Dryzek, J., Norgaard, R., Schlosberg, D., & Durham, (Eds.). Cary, North Carolina: Oxford University Press.
Chart with search: "Key Components of Climate Change Denial Machine."

We are now experiencing the sixth extinction...

Kolbert, E. (2014). *The Sixth Extinction: An Unnatural History*. New York: Henry Holt and Co.

66   **Please visit www.footprintnetwork.org, input...**

http://www.footprintnetwork.org

67   **The crying Native American commercial...**

Advertising Educational Foundation. (2003) *Pollution Prevention: Keep America Beautiful -- Iron Eyes Cody (1961 - 1983)*
http://www.aef.com/exhibits/social_responsibility/ad_council/2278

Commercial is an example of how empathic resonanc....

Berenguer, J. (2010). The effect of empathy in environmental moral reasoning. *Environment and Behavior*, 42 (1), 110-134.

Roszak, T., Gomes, M., Kanner, A., & Brown, L. (1995) *Ecopsychology: Restoring the Earth, Healing the Mind*. San Francisco, Sierra Club Books.

68   **If you were alive around 200 years ago...**

Shermer, M. (2014). *The Moral Arc: How Science and Reason Lead Humanity toward Truth, Justice, and Freedom*. New York: Henry Holt & Co.

70   **Trickle down economics has always been a...**

Piketty, T. (2014). *Capital in the Twenty-First Century*. Cambridge, MA: Belknap Press.

The well-intentioned idea of pluralistic relativism...

Harris, S. (2011). *The Moral Landscape: How Science Can Determine Values*. Washington, DC: Free Press

Pinker, S. (2002). *The Blank Slate: The Modern Denial of Human Nature*. New York: Viking Press.

Shweder, R. (2012). Relativism and Universalism. *A Companion to Moral Anthropology*. Fassin, D., Shweder, R. (Eds.), online: John Wiley & Sons, Inc.

85   **Blessed are the hearts that can bend; they shall never be...**

Zaretsky, R. (2013) *A Life Worth Living: Albert Camus and the Quest for Meaning*. Belknap Press.

87   **Every child is an artist. The problem is...**

Richardson, J. (2007). *A Life of Picasso: The Prodigy, 1881-1906*. New York: Knopf.

89 We are all going to die, all of us, what a circus!...

Bukowski, C., Crumb, R. (2002). *The Captain is Out to Lunch*. New York: Ecco.

92 We fear death in inverse proportion...

Yalom, I. (1980). *Existential Psychotherapy*. New York: Basic Books.

94 Don't be too timid and squeamish about your actions.

Emerson, R. W. (2000). *The Essential Writings of Ralph Waldo Emerson*. Atkinson, B. (Ed.) New York: Modern Library.

Luke Rhinehardt's, *The Dice Man*, a fictional cult...

Rhinehart, L. (1971). *The Dice Man*. New York: William Morrow.

95 The search for a singular self may also...

Lifton, R. (1993). *The Protean Self: Human Resilience in an Age of Fragmentation*. New York: Basic Books.

98 Out beyond ideas of wrongdoing and rightdoing...

Barks, Coleman, (2010). *Rumi: The Big Red Book: The Great Masterpiece Celebrating Mystical Love and Friendship*. New York: HarperOne.

much of our reasoning, including...

Khaneman, D. (2013). *Thinking, Fast and Slow*. New York: Farrar, Straus and Giroux.

Burton, R. (2009). *On Being Certain: Believing You Are Right Even When You're Not*. New York: St. Martin's Griffin.

103 There, but for the grace of God, go I.

Foxe, J. (2010). *Foxe's Book of Martyrs*. Eureka, Montana: Lighthouse Trails Publishing, LLC.

One use of the term radical acceptance...

Brach, T. (2003). *Radical Acceptance. Embracing Your Life With the Heart of a Buddha*. New York: Bantam.

104 John Rawls' *A Theory of Justice* proposes a method...

Rawls, J. (2005). *A Theory of Justice*. Boston, MA: Belknap Press of Harvard University Press.

106 Humility is not thinking less of oneself, but...

McGrath, A. (2013) *C. S. Lewis - A Life: Eccentric Genius, Reluctant Prophet*.

Carol Stream, IL: Tyndale House Publishers, Inc.

Naikan is a 500-year-old set of practices…

Reynolds, D. (1983). *Naikan Psychotherapy: Meditation for Self-Development.* Chicago, IL: University of Chicago.

This interpretive tendency is so prominent…

Khaneman, D. (2013). *Thinking, Fast and Slow.* New York: Farrar, Straus and Giroux.

111   **Modern research on the benefits of forgiveness…**

Worthington, E. (2001). *Five Steps to Forgiveness: The Art and Science of Forgiveness.* New York: Crown.

Luskin, F. (2003). *Forgive for Good.* New York: HarperOne.

113   **a lack of forgiveness and even the thirst for vengeance…**

Wright, R. (1994). *The Moral Animal: Why We Are, the Way We Are: The New Science of Evolutionary Psychology.* New York: Pantheon.

115   **The misery that people cling to is ego misery.**

Tolle, E. (1999). *The Power of Now: A Guide to Spiritual Enlightenment.* Novato, CA: New World Library.

Sarno, J. (2007). *The Divided Mind: The Epidemic of Mindbody Disorders.* New York: Harper Perennial.

121   **In Five Steps to Forgiveness: The Art and Science…**

Worthington, E. (2001). *Five Steps to Forgiveness: The Art and Science of Forgiveness.* New York: Crown.

Victor Frankl survived the German concentration

Frankl, V. (1959). *Man's Search for Meaning.* New York: Beacon.

124   **Treat the earth well, It was not given to you…**

http://www.legendsofamerica.com/na-proverbs.html

125   **Are you aware that listening to a one-sided…**

Galván, V., Vessal, R., Golley, M., (2013). The Effects of Cell Phone Conversations on the Attention and Memory of Bystanders. *PLoS ONE*, 8 (3).

126   **Deciding how many children to have…**

Overall, C. (2012). *Why Have Children?: The Ethical Debate.* Cambridge, MA: The MIT Press.

Archard, D. & Benatar, D. (2011). *Procreation and Parenthood: The Ethics of*

Bearing and Rearing Children, Cary, NC: Oxford University Press.

128   **My religion is kindness.**

Gyatso, T. & Cutler, H. (2009). *The Art of Happiness: A Handbook for Living.* New York: Riverhead Publishing.

LKM involves generating feelings of kindness...

Salzberg, S. (1995). *Lovingkindness: The Revolutionary Art of Happiness*, Boulder, CO: Shambhala.

Weibel, D. (2007). *A Novel Loving-Kindness Intervention: Boosting Compassion for Self and Others.* Dissertation Abstracts International.

130   **LKM excerpt:**

Weibel, D. (2007). *A Novel Loving-Kindness Intervention: Boosting Compassion for Self and Others.* Dissertation Abstracts International.

137   **Many persons have a wrong idea of what constitutes...**

Keller, H., Sullivan, A. (2011). *The Story Of My Life: With Her Letters (1887–1901) And A Supplementary Account Of Her Education, Including Passages From The Reports And Letters Of Her Teacher, Anne Mansfield Sullivan.* Charleston, South Carolina: Nabu Press.

There is a convincing body of research...

Post, S. & Neimark, J. (2007). *Why Good Things Happen to Good People: How to Live a Longer, Healthier, Happier Life by the Simple Act of Giving.* New York: Broadway Books.

Post, S. (2007). *Altruism and Health: Perspectives from Empirical Research.* Cary, NC: Oxford University Press.

144   **The leading altruism theorists believe altruism...**

Trivers, R. (1971). *The Evolution of Reciprocal Altruism. Quarterly Review of Biology*, 46: 35–57.

Axelrod, R. (1984). *The Evolution of Cooperation.* New York: Basic Books.

149   **Our task must be to free ourselves by widening our circle...**

Isaacson, W. (2008) *Einstein: His Life and Universe.* New York: Simon & Schuster

There are models that describe the path of expanding...

Beck, D. & Cowan, C. (1996). *Spiral Dynamics: Mastering Values, Leadership and Change.* New York: Blackwell Publishing.

Gilligan, C., Ward, J., Taylor, J. & Bardige, B. (1990). *Mapping the Moral Domain: A Contribution of Women's Thinking to Psychological Theory and Education.* Harvard University Press, MA.

Loevinger, J. (1987). *Paradigms of Personality*. New York: Freeman.

Maslow, A. (1971). *The Farther Reaches of Human Nature*. New York: Viking Press.

Wilber, K. (1995). *Sex, Ecology, & Spirituality: The Spirit of Evolution*. Boulder, CO: Shambhala Publications.

Wilber, K. (2000). *Integral Psychology*. Boulder, CO: Shambhala Publications.

161 **Some scholars also have intentionally or...**

Freeman, D. (1983). *Margaret Mead and Samoa*. Boston, MA: Harvard University Press.

165 **Calhoun, a senator from South Carolina rationalized...**

Calhoun, J. C. (1837). *The "Positive Good" of Slavery*, Speech in the United States Senate.

About the Author

David Weibel is a psychologist and student of life who helps remedy suffering and facilitate transcendence, sometimes even at the same time. He has practiced mindfulness and compassion for twenty years and has helped many people expand their perspective. He believes in play, both on the field, and in life. A brilliant professor lured him from San Francisco to Baton Rouge.